Introduction

D0289386

Friends,

During Lent, we apprentice to Jesus in his forty-day sojourn in the desert. We stubbornly stay with him, doing what he did there, facing what he faced there.

The desert is the place of clarification. When we have been stripped of the relatively trivial desires that preoccupy us, we can see, with a somewhat disturbing clarity, who we essentially are and what most pressingly matters. Blaise Pascal said that most of us spend our lives seeking *divertissements* (distractions), for we cannot bear the weight of the great questions. We play, gossip, eat and drink, seek the most banal entertainment—so that we don't have to face the truth about ourselves, the reality of death, and the demands of God. The Spirit drives holy people into the desert because it is the place where the *divertissements* disappear: "He fasted for forty days and forty nights."

At the end of the Lord's fast, the tempter arrives—because decision follows clarification. How often in Scripture the theme of decision arises. Jesus himself provokes the stark choice: "Whoever is not with me is against me, and whoever does not gather with me scatters."

And then Jesus is ready for mission; immediately after the temptations, he gathers his disciples around him and commences the ministry that will reach its culmination only on the cross.

So this Lent, let us resolve to rid ourselves of *divertissements*, going a bit hungry and thirsty, purposely running on empty—so that the great questions may be asked with clarity. Let us allow the devil to come, tempting us with the love of pleasure, the ego, and power—for in temptation comes decision. And in the desert with Jesus the Master, let us realize that we too are people on mission—because in decision comes identity.

Peace,

+ Robert Barron

Bishop Robert Barron

LENTEN
GOSPEL
REFLECTIONS

BISHOP ROBERT BARRON
with reflection questions by Peggy Pandaleon

WORD ON FIRE CATHOLIC MINISTRIES

www.WORDONFIRE.org

Excerpts from the Lectionary for Mass for use
in the dioceses of the United States of America,
second typical edition.

Copyright © 1970, 1986, 1997, 1998, 2001
Confraternity of Christian Doctrine, Inc., Washington, D.C.
All rights reserved.

No part of this work may be reproduced or transmitted in any form
or by any means, electronic or mechanical, including photocopying,
recording, or by any information storage and retrieval system,
without permission in writing from the copyright owner.

LENTEN

GOSPEL

REFLECTIONS

Wednesday, March 2, 2022

Ash Wednesday

MATTHEW 6:1-6,16-18

Jesus said to his disciples:
"Take care not to perform righteous deeds in order
that people may see them; otherwise, you will have
no recompense from your heavenly Father. When
you give alms, do not blow a trumpet before you,
as the hypocrites do in the synagogues and in the
streets to win the praise of others. Amen, I say to
you, they have received their reward. But when you
give alms, do not let your left hand know what your
right is doing, so that your almsgiving may be secret.
And your Father who sees in secret will repay you.

"When you pray, do not be like the hypocrites, who
love to stand and pray in the synagogues and on
street corners so that others may see them. Amen,
I say to you, they have received their reward. But
when you pray, go to your inner room, close the
door, and pray to your Father in secret. And your
Father who sees in secret will repay you.

"When you fast, do not look gloomy like the
hypocrites. They neglect their appearance, so that
they may appear to others to be fasting. Amen, I say
to you, they have received their reward. But when
you fast, anoint your head and wash your face, so

> that you may not appear to be fasting, except to
> your Father who is hidden. And your Father who
> sees what is hidden will repay you."

Friends, today's Gospel asks us to do three things: pray, fast, and give alms. Let's focus today on prayer. Studies show that prayer is a very common, very popular activity. Even those who profess no belief in God pray!

What is prayer, and how should we pray? Prayer is intimate communion and conversation with God. Judging from Jesus' own life, prayer is something that we ought to do often, especially at key moments of our lives.

Well, how should we pray? What does it look like? You have to pray with faith, and according to Jesus' model, you have to pray with forgiveness. The efficacy of prayer seems to depend on the reconciliation of differences.

You also have to pray with persistence. One reason that we don't receive what we want through prayer is that we give up too easily. Augustine said that God sometimes delays in giving us what we want because he wants our hearts to expand.

Finally, we have to pray in Jesus' name. In doing so we are relying on his influence with the Father, trusting that the Father will listen to him.

REFLECT: What can you do this Lent to strengthen your prayer life?

Thursday, March 3, 2022

Thursday after Ash Wednesday

LUKE 9:22-25

Jesus said to his disciples:
"The Son of Man must suffer greatly and be rejected by the elders, the chief priests, and the scribes, and be killed and on the third day be raised."

Then he said to all, "If anyone wishes to come after me, he must deny himself and take up his cross daily and follow me. For whoever wishes to save his life will lose it, but whoever loses his life for my sake will save it. What profit is there for one to gain the whole world yet lose or forfeit himself?"

Friends, our Gospel today lays out Jesus' conditions for discipleship. For all of us sinners, to varying degrees, our own lives have become god. That is to say, we see the universe turning around our ego, our needs, our projects, our plans, and our likes and dislikes. True conversion—the *metanoia* that Jesus talks about—is so much more than moral reform, though it includes that. It has to do with a complete shift in consciousness, a whole new way of looking at one's life.

Jesus offered a teaching that must have been gut-wrenching to his first-century audience: "If anyone wishes to come after me, he must deny himself and take up his cross daily and follow me." His listeners knew what the cross meant: a death in utter agony, nakedness, and humiliation. They didn't think of the cross automatically in religious terms, as we do. They knew it in all of its awful power.

Unless you crucify your ego, you cannot be my follower, Jesus says. This move—this terrible move—has to be the foundation of the spiritual life.

REFLECT: Where is your ego overly dominant? What do you have to do to crucify it?

Friday, March 4, 2022

Friday after Ash Wednesday

MATTHEW 9:14-15

The disciples of John approached Jesus and said, "Why do we and the Pharisees fast much, but your disciples do not fast?" Jesus answered them, "Can the wedding guests mourn as long as the bridegroom is with them? The days will come when the bridegroom is taken away from them, and then they will fast."

Friends, in today's Gospel, people ask Jesus why he and his disciples do not fast when John and his disciples do. Jesus' answer is wonderful: "Can the wedding guests mourn as long as the bridegroom is with them?" Could you imagine people fasting at a wedding banquet? It would be ridiculous!

Jesus later says, "People do not put new wine into old wineskins." The new wine is the Gospel. The receptacle for this wine must be conformed to it, not the other way around.

To take in the Good News, we can't be living in the cramped space of our sinful souls. We can't have an "expect the worst" attitude. Instead we *repent*, or change the minds that we have. Another way to get at this is to say that like is known by like. If God is love, then only a soul that is on fire with love will properly take him in.

REFLECT: When is the appropriate time to fast? When is the appropriate time to feast?

Saturday, March 5, 2022

Saturday after Ash Wednesday

LUKE 5:27-32

Jesus saw a tax collector named Levi sitting at the customs post. He said to him, "Follow me." And leaving everything behind, he got up and followed him. Then Levi gave a great banquet for him in his house, and a large crowd of tax collectors and others were at table with them. The Pharisees and their scribes complained to his disciples, saying, "Why do you eat and drink with tax collectors and sinners?" Jesus said to them in reply, "Those who are healthy do not need a physician, but the sick do. I have not come to call the righteous to repentance but sinners."

Friends, today's Gospel tells the story of the Lord calling Levi, also known as Matthew. As Jesus was passing by, he spotted Matthew at his tax collector's post. To be a tax collector in Jesus' time—a Jew collaborating with Rome's oppression of one's own people—was to be a contemptible figure.

Jesus gazed at Matthew and simply said, "Follow me." Did Jesus invite Matthew because the tax collector merited it? Was Jesus responding to a request from Matthew or some longing in the sinner's heart? Certainly not. Grace, by definition, comes unbidden and without explanation.

In Caravaggio's magnificent painting of this scene, Matthew, dressed anachronistically in sixteenth-century finery, responds to Jesus' summons by pointing incredulously to himself and wearing a quizzical expression, as if to say, "Me? You want me?"

Just as creation is *ex nihilo*, so conversion is a new creation, a gracious remaking of a person from the nonbeing of his sin. Matthew, we are told, immediately got up and followed the Lord.

REFLECT: Reflect on a time when grace came to you "unbidden and without explanation."

Sunday, March 6, 2022

First Sunday of Lent

LUKE 4:1-13

Filled with the Holy Spirit, Jesus returned from the Jordan and was led by the Spirit into the desert for forty days, to be tempted by the devil. He ate nothing during those days, and when they were over he was hungry. The devil said to him, "If you are the Son of God, command this stone to become bread." Jesus answered him, "It is written, *One does not live on bread alone.*" Then he took him up and showed him all the kingdoms of the world in a single instant. The devil said to him, "I shall give to you all this power and glory; for it has been handed over to me, and I may give it to whomever I wish. All this will be yours, if you worship me." Jesus said to him in reply, "It is written

> *You shall worship the Lord, your God,*
> *and him alone shall you serve.*"

Then he led him to Jerusalem, made him stand on the parapet of the temple, and said to him, "If you are the Son of God, throw yourself down from here, for it is written:

> *He will command his angels concerning you,*
> *to guard you,*

and:

> *With their hands they will support you,*
> *lest you dash your foot against a stone."*

Jesus said to him in reply, "It also says, *You shall not put the Lord, your God, to the test.*" When the devil had finished every temptation, he departed from him for a time.

Friends, in our Gospel for the First Sunday of Lent, Luke gives us the story of the temptation in the desert. At every point in the Gospels, we are meant to identify with Jesus. God became man that man might become God. We participate in him and thereby learn what a godly life is like.

Jesus has just been baptized; he has just learned his deepest identity and mission. And now he confronts—as we all must—the great temptations. What precisely is entailed in being the beloved Son of God?

First, the tempter urges him to use his divine power to satisfy his bodily desires, which Jesus dismisses with a word. Having failed at his first attempt, the devil shifts to perhaps the greatest of the temptations: power. Power is extremely seductive. Many would gladly eschew material things or attention or fame in order to get it. Jesus' great answer in Matthew's account of this story is "Get away, Satan!" To seek power is to serve Satan—it is stated that bluntly.

Finally, the devil plays a subtler game—he tempts Jesus to manipulate his Father, encouraging him to jump from the temple and let angels save him. It is the temptation faced by Adam and Eve in the garden: deciding how and when God will act.

REFLECT: What is the difference between seeking power and having power? When you have power, how should you use it so that you do not serve Satan?

Monday, March 7, 2022

First Week of Lent

MATTHEW 25:31-46

Jesus said to his disciples:
"When the Son of Man comes in his glory, and all the angels with him, he will sit upon his glorious throne, and all the nations will be assembled before him. And he will separate them one from another, as a shepherd separates the sheep from the goats. He will place the sheep on his right and the goats on his left. Then the king will say to those on his right, 'Come, you who are blessed by my Father. Inherit the kingdom prepared for you from the foundation of the world. For I was hungry and you gave me food, I was thirsty and you gave me drink, a stranger and you welcomed me, naked and you clothed me, ill and you cared for me, in prison and you visited me.' Then the righteous will answer him and say, 'Lord, when did we see you hungry and feed you, or thirsty and give you drink? When did we see you a stranger and welcome you, or naked and clothe you? When did we see you ill or in prison, and visit you?' And the king will say to them in reply, 'Amen, I say to you, whatever you did for one of these least brothers of mine, you did for me.' Then he will say to those on his left, 'Depart from me, you accursed, into the eternal fire prepared for

the Devil and his angels. For I was hungry and you gave me no food, I was thirsty and you gave me no drink, a stranger and you gave me no welcome, naked and you gave me no clothing, ill and in prison, and you did not care for me.' Then they will answer and say, 'Lord, when did we see you hungry or thirsty or a stranger or naked or ill or in prison, and not minister to your needs?' He will answer them, 'Amen, I say to you, what you did not do for one of these least ones, you did not do for me.' And these will go off to eternal punishment, but the righteous to eternal life."

Friends, in our Gospel today, Jesus tells the crowd that the Son of Man will welcome the righteous into the kingdom, saying, "For I was hungry and you gave me food, I was thirsty and you gave me drink, a stranger and you welcomed me, naked and you clothed me, ill and you cared for me, in prison and you visited me." Puzzled, the righteous will ask when they did this, and he will reply, "Whatever you did for one of these least brothers of mine, you did for me."

This is a powerful evocation of Jesus' teaching about the mutuality of our love for God and neighbor. The absolute love for God is not in competition with a radical commitment to love our fellow human beings, precisely because God is not one being among many, but the very ground of our existence.

Someone who operated very much in the spirit of this teaching was St. Teresa of Kolkata. A writer was once conversing with her, searching out the sources of her spirituality and mission. At the end of their long talk, she asked him to spread his hand out on the table. Touching his fingers one by one as she spoke the words, she said, "You did it to me."

REFLECT: Is it possible to love God and not have love for some people? Why is this a serious contradiction?

Tuesday, March 8, 2022

First Week of Lent

MATTHEW 6:7-15

Jesus said to his disciples:
"In praying, do not babble like the pagans, who think that they will be heard because of their many words. Do not be like them. Your Father knows what you need before you ask him.

"This is how you are to pray:

> Our Father who art in heaven,
> hallowed be thy name,
> thy Kingdom come,
> thy will be done,
> on earth as it is in heaven.
> Give us this day our daily bread;
> and forgive us our trespasses,
> as we forgive those who trespass against us;
> and lead us not into temptation,
> but deliver us from evil.

"If you forgive men their transgressions, your heavenly Father will forgive you. But if you do not forgive men, neither will your Father forgive your transgressions."

Friends, the Gospel for today is of great significance, for in it the Son of God teaches us to pray. We hear from not just a guru, a spiritual teacher, or a religious genius, but from the very Son of God. This is why the Our Father, the Lord's Prayer, is the model of all prayer.

The Lord's Prayer is the prayer for the Christian journey which has been offered up consistently for the past two thousand years. Think for a moment how this prayer links us to all of the great figures in Christian history, from Peter and Paul to Augustine, Thomas Aquinas, Francis of Assisi, John Henry Newman, G.K. Chesterton, John Paul II, and right up to the present day.

Keep in mind that prayer is not designed so much to change God's mind or to tell God something he doesn't know. God isn't like a big city boss or a reluctant pasha whom we have to persuade. Rather, he is the one who wants nothing other than to give us good things—though they might not always be the things we want.

REFLECT: How is "thy will be done" a critical part of the Lord's Prayer? When you pray, can you truly surrender the outcome to God?

Wednesday, March 9, 2022

First Week of Lent

While still more people gathered in the crowd, Jesus said to them, "This generation is an evil generation; it seeks a sign, but no sign will be given it, except the sign of Jonah. Just as Jonah became a sign to the Ninevites, so will the Son of Man be to this generation. At the judgment the queen of the south will rise with the men of this generation and she will condemn them, because she came from the ends of the earth to hear the wisdom of Solomon, and there is something greater than Solomon here. At the judgment the men of Nineveh will arise with this generation and condemn it, because at the preaching of Jonah they repented, and there is something greater than Jonah here."

Friends, in today's Gospel, Jesus tells the crowd that they will receive no sign except the sign of Jonah, which was a prophetic code for his death and Resurrection.

Everything Jesus said and did, in one way or another, is an anticipation of his Resurrection. The God of Israel, the God of Jesus Christ, is a God of life, a God of the living. He hates death and the ways of death.

He hates sin, which brings about spiritual death; he hates physical illness, which brings about bodily death; he hates corruption, which brings about societal death. And so he battles all these things all the way. Jesus heals blind eyes and deaf ears and crippled limbs; he illuminates darkened minds; he liberates imprisoned souls.

His ministry is a ministry of life, of the triumph of life over death.

REFLECT: In what ways does the Church continue Jesus' ministry of life? Do you embrace all the Church's life-giving teachings?

Thursday, March 10, 2022

First Week of Lent

MATTHEW 7:7-12

Jesus said to his disciples:
"Ask and it will be given to you; seek and you will find; knock and the door will be opened to you. For everyone who asks, receives; and the one who seeks, finds; and to the one who knocks, the door will be opened. Which one of you would hand his son a stone when he asked for a loaf of bread, or a snake when he asked for a fish? If you then, who are wicked, know how to give good gifts to your children, how much more will your heavenly Father give good things to those who ask him.

"Do to others whatever you would have them do to you. This is the law and the prophets."

Friends, today's Gospel assures us of the power of prayer. When some people ask in a spirit of trust, really believing that what they are asking for will happen, it happens. Just as Jesus suggests in the Gospel, "Everyone who asks, receives; and the one who seeks, finds; and to the one who knocks, the door will be opened."

The power of prayer is the confidence that we are being guided and cared for, even when that guidance and care are not immediately apparent. It is what allows someone to live in detachment from all of the ups and downs of life. In the language of St. Ignatius of Loyola: "We should not prefer health to sickness, riches to poverty, honor to dishonor, a long life to a short life. . . . Our one desire and choice should be what is more conducive to the end for which we are created . . . to praise, reverence, and serve God our Lord."

Someone that lives in that kind of detachment is free, and because they are free, they are powerful. They are beyond the threats that arise in the context of this world. This is the source of *dynamis*, real power. This is the power that Martin Luther King Jr., Dorothy Day, and John Paul II wielded: world-changing power.

REFLECT: How can prayer be both active ("ask, seek, knock") and also detached? What is the source of this detachment?

Friday, March 11, 2022

First Week of Lent

MATTHEW 5:20-26

Jesus said to his disciples: "I tell you, unless your righteousness surpasses that of the scribes and Pharisees, you will not enter into the Kingdom of heaven.

"You have heard that it was said to your ancestors, *You shall not kill; and whoever kills will be liable to judgment.* But I say to you, whoever is angry with his brother will be liable to judgment, and whoever says to his brother, *Raqa*, will be answerable to the Sanhedrin, and whoever says, 'You fool,' will be liable to fiery Gehenna. Therefore, if you bring your gift to the altar, and there recall that your brother has anything against you, leave your gift there at the altar, go first and be reconciled with your brother, and then come and offer your gift. Settle with your opponent quickly while on the way to court. Otherwise your opponent will hand you over to the judge, and the judge will hand you over to the guard, and you will be thrown into prison. Amen, I say to you, you will not be released until you have paid the last penny."

Friends, in today's Gospel, Jesus commands us to be reconciled with one another. I want to say something about the role of forgiveness in repairing our broken relationships.

When you are at worship and realize that you need to forgive someone (or be forgiven by someone), go and do it. Go get reconciled, then come back. It's like a rule of physics. There is something hidden in the deep mystery of God, and I can't fully explicate it. Somehow, if there is a lack of forgiveness in you, it blocks the movement of God in you. Perhaps it's simply because God is love, and so whatever is opposed to love in us blocks the flow of God's power and God's life.

One reason we do not forgive is that we feel that some injustice has been done to us, and we resent it. A good cure for this feeling is to kneel before the cross of Jesus. What do you see there? The innocent Son of God nailed to the cross—the ultimate injustice. What does he do? He forgives his persecutors. Meditate on that, and your sense of being treated unjustly will fade away.

REFLECT: Reflect on a time when you have truly been treated unjustly. How can the Passion of Jesus help you forgive and move on from that injustice?

Saturday, March 12, 2022

First Week of Lent

MATTHEW 5:43-48

Jesus said to his disciples: "You have heard that it was said, *You shall love your neighbor and hate your enemy.* But I say to you, love your enemies, and pray for those who persecute you, that you may be children of your heavenly Father, for he makes his sun rise on the bad and the good, and causes rain to fall on the just and the unjust. For if you love those who love you, what recompense will you have? Do not the tax collectors do the same? And if you greet your brothers and sisters only, what is unusual about that? Do not the pagans do the same? So be perfect, just as your heavenly Father is perfect."

Friends, today's Gospel tells us to love our enemies so that we may be like the Father. What is the Father of Jesus Christ like? Well, listen: "He makes his sun rise on the bad and the good, and causes rain to fall on the just and the unjust."

In every case, his grace comes first, and grace is all that he has to give. This is why the comparison to the sun and the rain is so apt. The sun doesn't ask who deserves its warmth or its light before it shines. It just shines, and both good and bad people receive it. Neither does the rain inquire as to the moral rectitude of those upon whom it showers its life-giving goodness. It just pours—and both just and unjust people receive it.

REFLECT: Have you ever asked God to give you the grace to love "unlovable" people the way he loves them? If so, what happened? If not, why do you want to hang on to your negativity?

Sunday, March 13, 2022

Second Sunday of Lent

LUKE 9:28B-36

Jesus took Peter, John, and James and went up the mountain to pray. While he was praying his face changed in appearance and his clothing became dazzling white. And behold, two men were conversing with him, Moses and Elijah, who appeared in glory and spoke of his exodus that he was going to accomplish in Jerusalem. Peter and his companions had been overcome by sleep, but becoming fully awake, they saw his glory and the two men standing with him. As they were about to part from him, Peter said to Jesus, "Master, it is good that we are here; let us make three tents, one for you, one for Moses, and one for Elijah." But he did not know what he was saying. While he was still speaking, a cloud came and cast a shadow over them, and they became frightened when they entered the cloud. Then from the cloud came a voice that said, "This is my chosen Son; listen to him." After the voice had spoken, Jesus was found alone. They fell silent and did not at that time tell anyone what they had seen.

Friends, today's Gospel recounts the story of the Transfiguration. Here, the glorified Jesus represents the fulfillment of the Old Testament revelation, symbolized by Moses, representing the Law, and Elijah, representing the prophets.

Let's look at the two basic divisions. God gave the Torah, the Law, to his people, in order that they might become a priestly people, a holy nation, a people set apart, in the hopes that they would then function as a sort of magnet to the rest of the world. But the Law didn't take. From the very beginning, the people turned away from its dictates and became as bad as the nations around them.

And then the prophets. Over and again we hear the call to be faithful to the Torah, to follow the ways of the Lord. The prophets turn on Israel itself repeatedly, reminding her of her sinfulness.

And then came Jesus, God and man. Jesus did what no hero of Judaism had ever done: fulfilled the Law, remained utterly obedient to the demands of the Father, even to the point of laying down his life. He brought the Torah and the prophets thereby to fulfillment.

REFLECT: How is it that even though we are sinners, we can also be transfigured and glorified if we live in and through Jesus?

Monday, March 14, 2022

Second Week of Lent

LUKE 6:36-38

Jesus said to his disciples:
"Be merciful, just as your Father is merciful.

"Stop judging and you will not be judged. Stop condemning and you will not be condemned. Forgive and you will be forgiven. Give and gifts will be given to you; a good measure, packed together, shaken down, and overflowing, will be poured into your lap. For the measure with which you measure will in return be measured out to you."

Friends, in today's Gospel, Jesus calls us to "be merciful, just as your Father is merciful."

Mercy or tender compassion (*chesed* in the Hebrew of the Old Testament) is God's most distinctive characteristic. St. Augustine reminded us that we are, by our very nature, ordered to God. But since God is tender mercy, "having" God is tantamount to exercising compassion, being merciful ourselves.

And attend to what Jesus says next: "Stop judging and you will not be judged. Stop condemning and you will not be condemned. Forgive and you will be forgiven. Give and gifts will be given to you." According to the "physics" of the spiritual order, the more one draws on the divine life, the more one receives that life, precisely because it is a gift and is properly infinite. God's life is had, as it were, on the fly: when you receive it as a gift, you must give it away, since it only exists in gift form, and then you will find more of it flooding into your heart.

If you want to be happy, Jesus is saying, this divine love, this chesed of God, must be central to your life; it must be your beginning, your middle, and your end

REFLECT: How have you "regifted" God's love? When are you tempted to hang on to it and not give it away?

Tuesday, March 15, 2022

Second Week of Lent

MATTHEW 23:1-12

Jesus spoke to the crowds and to his disciples, saying, "The scribes and the Pharisees have taken their seat on the chair of Moses. Therefore, do and observe all things whatsoever they tell you, but do not follow their example. For they preach but they do not practice. They tie up heavy burdens hard to carry and lay them on people's shoulders, but they will not lift a finger to move them. All their works are performed to be seen. They widen their phylacteries and lengthen their tassels. They love places of honor at banquets, seats of honor in synagogues, greetings in marketplaces, and the salutation 'Rabbi.' As for you, do not be called 'Rabbi.' You have but one teacher, and you are all brothers. Call no one on earth your father; you have but one Father in heaven. Do not be called 'Master'; you have but one master, the Christ. The greatest among you must be your servant. Whoever exalts himself will be humbled; but whoever humbles himself will be exalted."

Friends, today's Gospel exposes the pride of the Pharisees and concludes with the prescription of humility. I want to reflect on this virtue.

St. Augustine said that all of us, made from nothing, tend toward nothing. We can see this in our frailty and sin and mortality. St. Paul said, "What do you possess that you have not received? But if you have received it, why are you boasting as if you did not receive it?"

To believe in God is to know these truths. To live them out is to live in the attitude of humility. Thomas Aquinas said *humilitas veritas*, meaning "humility is truth." It is living out the deepest truth of things: God is God and we are not.

Now, all of this sounds very clear when it's stated in this abstract manner, but man is it hard to live out! In our fallen world, we forget so readily that we are creatures. We start to assume that we are gods, the center of the universe.

The ego becomes a massive monkey on our backs, and it has to be fed and pampered constantly. What a liberation it is to let go of the ego! Do you see why humility is not a degradation but an elevation?

REFLECT: Reflect on how pride becomes a burden and how humility frees and elevates.

_____

_____

_____

_____

_____

Wednesday, March 16, 2022

Second Week of Lent

MATTHEW 20:17-28

As Jesus was going up to Jerusalem, he took the Twelve disciples aside by themselves, and said to them on the way, "Behold, we are going up to Jerusalem, and the Son of Man will be handed over to the chief priests and the scribes, and they will condemn him to death, and hand him over to the Gentiles to be mocked and scourged and crucified, and he will be raised on the third day."

Then the mother of the sons of Zebedee approached Jesus with her sons and did him homage, wishing to ask him for something. He said to her, "What do you wish?" She answered him, "Command that these two sons of mine sit, one at your right and the other at your left, in your kingdom." Jesus said in reply, "You do not know what you are asking. Can you drink the chalice that I am going to drink?" They said to him, "We can." He replied, "My chalice you will indeed drink, but to sit at my right and at my left, this is not mine to give but is for those for whom it has been prepared by my Father." When the ten heard this, they became indignant at the two brothers. But Jesus summoned them and said, "You know that the rulers of the Gentiles lord it over

> them, and the great ones make their authority over them felt. But it shall not be so among you. Rather, whoever wishes to be great among you shall be your servant; whoever wishes to be first among you shall be your slave. Just so, the Son of Man did not come to be served but to serve and to give his life as a ransom for many."

Friends, today in our Gospel, the mother of James and John asks Jesus on their behalf for high places of authority in his kingdom. Ah, there is the voice of ambition. Some people don't care at all about money or power or pleasure—but they care passionately about honor. A lot of people can identify with James and John. They want to go places, they want to be movers and shakers in society. Perhaps a number of people reading this reflection are filled with these emotions.

But Jesus turns the tables on them: "You do not know what you are asking." He is indeed a King, and he will indeed rule Israel, but his crown will be made of thorns, and his throne will be a Roman instrument of torture.

And so he tries to clarify: "Can you drink the chalice that I am going to drink?" The key to honor in the kingdom of God is to drink the cup of suffering, to be willing to suffer out of love, to give one's life away as a gift. Look at the lives of the saints. It is not about aggrandizing the ego but emptying it out.

REFLECT: How have you suffered out of love or given your life away as a gift?

_____

_____

_____

_____

_____

_____

_____

_____

_____

_____

_____

_____

_____

_____

_____

_____

Thursday, March 17, 2022

Second Week of Lent

LUKE 16:19-31

Jesus said to the Pharisees: "There was a rich man who dressed in purple garments and fine linen and dined sumptuously each day. And lying at his door was a poor man named Lazarus, covered with sores, who would gladly have eaten his fill of the scraps that fell from the rich man's table. Dogs even used to come and lick his sores. When the poor man died, he was carried away by angels to the bosom of Abraham. The rich man also died and was buried, and from the netherworld, where he was in torment, he raised his eyes and saw Abraham far off and Lazarus at his side. And he cried out, 'Father Abraham, have pity on me. Send Lazarus to dip the tip of his finger in water and cool my tongue, for I am suffering torment in these flames.' Abraham replied, 'My child, remember that you received what was good during your lifetime while Lazarus likewise received what was bad; but now he is comforted here, whereas you are tormented. Moreover, between us and you a great chasm is established to prevent anyone from crossing who might wish to go from our side to yours or from your side to ours.' He said, 'Then I beg you, father, send him to my father's house, for I have five brothers, so that he may warn them, lest they too come to this place of torment.' But Abraham replied, 'They have Moses and the prophets. Let them listen to them.' He said, 'Oh no, father Abraham, but if someone from the dead goes to them, they will repent.' Then Abraham said, 'If they will not listen to Moses and the prophets, neither will they be persuaded if someone should rise from the dead.'"

Friends, today's Gospel focuses on the parable of the rich man and Lazarus. The rich man "dressed in purple garments and fine linen and dined sumptuously each day," while lying at his door was a poor man named Lazarus, "who would gladly have eaten his fill of the scraps that fell from the rich man's table."

God is not pleased with this kind of economic inequality, and he burns with a passion to set things right. This theme came roaring up out of the Bible and into the Christian tradition, and it echoes up and down the centuries. Even though it makes us uncomfortable—and God knows it does, especially those of us who live in the most affluent society in the world—we can't avoid it, because it's everywhere in the Bible.

St. Thomas Aquinas says that we must distinguish between ownership and use of private property. We have a right to ownership through our hard work, through our inheritance. Fair enough. But with regard to the use of those things—how we use them, why we use them—then, says Thomas, we must always be concerned first for the common good and not our own. This especially includes Lazarus at our gate: those who are suffering and most in need.

REFLECT: In keeping with biblical teaching, how are you using your material things for the common good?

Friday, March 18, 2022

Second Week of Lent

MATTHEW 21:33-43, 45-46

Jesus said to the chief priests and the elders of the people: "Hear another parable. There was a landowner who planted a vineyard, put a hedge around it, dug a wine press in it, and built a tower. Then he leased it to tenants and went on a journey. When vintage time drew near, he sent his servants to the tenants to obtain his produce. But the tenants seized the servants and one they beat, another they killed, and a third they stoned. Again he sent other servants, more numerous than the first ones, but they treated them in the same way. Finally, he sent his son to them, thinking, 'They will respect my son.' But when the tenants saw the son, they said to one another, 'This is the heir. Come, let us kill him and acquire his inheritance.' They seized him, threw him out of the vineyard, and killed him. What will the owner of the vineyard do to those tenants when he comes?" They answered him, "He will put those wretched men to a wretched death and lease his vineyard to other tenants who will give him the produce at the proper times." Jesus said to them, "Did you never read in the Scriptures:

The stone that the builders rejected
*   has become the cornerstone;*

> *by the Lord has this been done,*
> *and it is wonderful in our eyes?*
>
> Therefore, I say to you, the Kingdom of God will
> be taken away from you and given to a people that
> will produce its fruit." When the chief priests and
> the Pharisees heard his parables, they knew that he
> was speaking about them. And although they were
> attempting to arrest him, they feared the crowds, for
> they regarded him as a prophet.

Friends, our Gospel today recounts the parable of the landowner who planted a vineyard and leased it to tenants. God is the landowner, the vineyard is his creation, and we are the tenants, responsible for caring for it.

In Jesus' telling of the story, the servants that the landowner sent to obtain his produce are the prophets and teachers of Israel, those who remind the people of their responsibilities toward God. But the tenants beat one servant, killed another, and stoned a third.

Finally, the landowner sent his son, expecting the tenants to respect him. So Jesus came, that we might direct the whole of our lives back to God, that we might remember that we are tenants and that the whole of the world belongs to God.

"But when the tenants saw the son . . . they seized him, threw him out of the vineyard and killed him." Here, of course, is the whole tragedy of Jesus' cross. When God sent his Son to us, we killed him. This is the insane resistance to God's intentions which is called sin.

REFLECT: In what ways are you sensitive to the responsibility of caring for God's creation?

Saturday, March 19, 2022

Solemnity of Saint Joseph, Spouse of the Blessed Virgin Mary

MATTHEW 1:16, 18-21, 24A (OR LUKE 2:41-51A)

Jacob was the father of Joseph, the husband of Mary. Of her was born Jesus who is called the Christ.

Now this is how the birth of Jesus Christ came about. When his mother Mary was betrothed to Joseph, but before they lived together, she was found with child through the Holy Spirit. Joseph her husband, since he was a righteous man, yet unwilling to expose her to shame, decided to divorce her quietly. Such was his intention when, behold, the angel of the Lord appeared to him in a dream and said, "Joseph, son of David, do not be afraid to take Mary your wife into your home. For it is through the Holy Spirit that this child has been conceived in her. She will bear a son and you are to name him Jesus, because he will save his people from their sins." When Joseph awoke, he did as the angel of the Lord had commanded him and took his wife into his home.

Friends, today we celebrate the feast of St. Joseph.

Every episode of Joseph's life is a crisis. He discovers that the woman to whom he was betrothed was pregnant. He resolved to divorce her quietly, but then the angel of the Lord appeared in a dream and explained the anomalous pregnancy. So Joseph understood what was happening in the context of God's providence and he took Mary as his wife.

Next, discovering that the child was in mortal danger, Joseph took mother and baby on a perilous journey to an unknown country. Anyone who has ever been forced to move to a new city knows something of the anxiety that Joseph must have felt. But Joseph went because God had commanded him.

Finally, we hear of Joseph desperately seeking his lost twelve-year-old son. Quietly taking the child home, Joseph once more put aside his human feelings and trusted in the purposes of God.

The little we know about Joseph is that he experienced heartbreak, fear unto death, and a parent's deepest anxiety. But each time, he read what happened to him as a theo-drama, not an ego-drama. This shift in attitude is what made Joseph the patron of the universal Church.

REFLECT: How can you have the trust of Joseph, especially in crisis?

Sunday, March 20, 2022

Third Sunday of Lent

LUKE 13:1-9

Some people told Jesus about the Galileans whose blood Pilate had mingled with the blood of their sacrifices. Jesus said to them in reply, "Do you think that because these Galileans suffered in this way they were greater sinners than all other Galileans? By no means! But I tell you, if you do not repent, you will all perish as they did! Or those eighteen people who were killed when the tower at Siloam fell on them—do you think they were more guilty than everyone else who lived in Jerusalem? By no means! But I tell you, if you do not repent, you will all perish as they did!"

And he told them this parable: "There once was a person who had a fig tree planted in his orchard, and when he came in search of fruit on it but found none, he said to the gardener, 'For three years now I have come in search of fruit on this fig tree but have found none. So cut it down. Why should it exhaust the soil?' He said to him in reply, 'Sir, leave it for this year also, and I shall cultivate the ground around it and fertilize it; it may bear fruit in the future. If not you can cut it down.'"

Friends, today's Gospel includes the parable of a fig tree that bears no fruit.

This is a standard trope in the theological literature of Israel: the tree that bears no fruit is evocative of the moral person who bears no spiritual fruit. Every single person has a mission: to be a conduit of the divine grace into the world. Planted in God— think of Jesus' image of the vine and the branches—they are meant to bring forth the fruits of love, peace, compassion, justice, nonviolence.

And notice that this should be effortless. The closer God gets, the more alive we become. But the mystery of sin is that we resist the invasion of God; we prefer to go our own way; we cling to our own prerogatives and our own narrow freedom. And the result is lifelessness. It feels like depression, like your life is going nowhere—in Dante's language, like being "lost in a dark wood."

In Jesus' parable, the one caring for the tree begs the owner for one more chance to "cultivate the ground around [the tree] and fertilize it," hoping to bring it back to life. But if no life comes, the tree will be cut down. This is the note of urgency that is struck over and again in the Bible. We can run out of time. We can become so resistant to God's grace that our leaves dry up. This is not divine vengeance; it is spiritual physics.

So don't be afraid of God! Surrender to him.

REFLECT: What does the lesson of the barren fig tree teach us about what is important in God's mind? Why is being morally upright not enough?

Monday, March 21, 2022

Third Week of Lent

LUKE 4:24-30

Jesus said to the people in the synagogue at Nazareth: "Amen, I say to you, no prophet is accepted in his own native place. Indeed, I tell you, there were many widows in Israel in the days of Elijah when the sky was closed for three and a half years and a severe famine spread over the entire land. It was to none of these that Elijah was sent, but only to a widow in Zarephath in the land of Sidon. Again, there were many lepers in Israel during the time of Elisha the prophet; yet not one of them was cleansed, but only Naaman the Syrian." When the people in the synagogue heard this, they were all filled with fury. They rose up, drove him out of the town, and led him to the brow of the hill on which their town had been built, to hurl him down headlong. But he passed through the midst of them and went away.

Friends, in today's Gospel, Jesus' hometown rejects him as a prophet. And I want to say a word about your role as a prophet.

When most lay people hear about prophecy, they sit back and their eyes glaze over: "That's something for the priests and the bishops to worry about; they're the modern-day prophets. I don't have that call or that responsibility."

Well, think again! Vatican II emphasized the universal call to holiness, rooted in the dynamics of baptism. Every baptized person is conformed unto Christ—priest, prophet, and king. Whenever you assist at Mass, you are exercising your priestly office, participating in the worship of God. Whenever you direct your kids to discover their mission in the Church, or provide guidance to someone in the spiritual life, you are exercising your kingly office.

As a baptized individual, you are also commissioned as a prophet—which is to say, a speaker of God's truth. And the prophetic word is not your own. It is not the result of your own meditations on the spiritual life, as valuable and correct as those may be. The prophetic word is the word of God given to you by God.

REFLECT: What is necessary for you to become a "speaker of God's truth"? What is holding you back?

Tuesday, March 22, 2022

Third Week of Lent

MATTHEW 18:21-35

Peter approached Jesus and asked him, "Lord, if my brother sins against me, how often must I forgive him? As many as seven times?" Jesus answered, "I say to you, not seven times but seventy-seven times. That is why the Kingdom of heaven may be likened to a king who decided to settle accounts with his servants. When he began the accounting, a debtor was brought before him who owed him a huge amount. Since he had no way of paying it back, his master ordered him to be sold, along with his wife, his children, and all his property, in payment of the debt. At that, the servant fell down, did him homage, and said, 'Be patient with me, and I will pay you back in full.' Moved with compassion the master of that servant let him go and forgave him the loan. When that servant had left, he found one of his fellow servants who owed him a much smaller amount. He seized him and started to choke him, demanding, 'Pay back what you owe.' Falling to his knees, his fellow servant begged him, 'Be patient with me, and I will pay you back.' But he refused. Instead, he had him put in prison until he paid back the debt. Now when his fellow servants saw what had happened, they were deeply disturbed, and went to their master and reported the whole affair. His master summoned him and said to him, 'You wicked servant! I forgave you your entire debt because you begged me to. Should you not have had pity on your fellow servant, as I had pity on you?' Then in anger his master handed him over to the torturers until he should pay back the whole debt. So will my heavenly Father do to you, unless each of you forgives your brother from your heart."

Friends, our Gospel today focuses on the gift of forgiveness. This is such an anchor of the New Testament and so central to Jesus' ministry and preaching. When it comes to the offenses that we have received from others, we are, all of us, great avatars of justice. We will remember every insult, every snub, and every shortcoming when it comes to our being hurt by others. That's why forgiving even once or twice is so difficult.

Forgiving seven times, as Peter suggests, is beyond the pale. Yet Jesus says to him, "I say to you, not seven times but seventy-seven times." In other words, forgive constantly, relentlessly, and without calculation. Your whole life must become an act of forgiveness.

And this is why Jesus tells the parable in today's Gospel. The man who had been forgiven so much should, at the very least, show forgiveness to the one who owed him so much less.

Here is the spiritual heart of the matter: whatever anyone owes you (in strict justice) is infinitely less than what God has graciously given to you; the divine forgiveness of you is infinitely greater than any forgiveness you might be called upon to offer.

Becoming an instrument of God's life, grace, forgiveness, and peace is what it is all about. Allow to flow through you what has been poured into you—that is the whole story.

REFLECT: Is there anyone you need to forgive? Reflect on God's mercy toward you as you plan a way to rebuild that relationship.

Wednesday, March 23, 2022

Third Week of Lent

Jesus said to his disciples: "Do not think that I have come to abolish the law or the prophets. I have come not to abolish but to fulfill. Amen, I say to you, until heaven and earth pass away, not the smallest letter or the smallest part of a letter will pass from the law, until all things have taken place. Therefore, whoever breaks one of the least of these commandments and teaches others to do so will be called least in the Kingdom of heaven. But whoever obeys and teaches these commandments will be called greatest in the Kingdom of heaven."

Friends, in our Gospel today, Jesus declares that he would not undermine the Law and the prophets but fulfill them. Jesus himself was an observant Jew, and the themes and images of the Holy Scriptures were elemental for him.

But what is he going to fulfill? Protestant theologian N.T. Wright has pointed out that the Old Testament is essentially an unfinished symphony, a drama without a climax. It is the articulation of a hope, a dream, a longing—but without a realization of that hope, without a satisfaction of that longing.

Israel knew itself to be the people with the definite mission to become holy and thereby to render the world holy. But instead, Israel fell into greater and greater sins, and instead of being the catalyst for the conversion of the world, the world was continually overwhelming and enslaving Israel.

And then came Jesus, who turned out to be, in the most unexpected way, the fulfillment of the dream. From the beginning of his ministry, Jesus effected the gathering of the tribes of Israel through conversion and the forgiveness of sins.

REFLECT: What are your hopes, dreams, and longings? How does Jesus fulfill them?

Thursday, March 24, 2022

Third Week of Lent

LUKE 11:14-23

Jesus was driving out a demon that was mute, and when the demon had gone out, the mute man spoke and the crowds were amazed. Some of them said, "By the power of Beelzebul, the prince of demons, he drives out demons." Others, to test him, asked him for a sign from heaven. But he knew their thoughts and said to them, "Every kingdom divided against itself will be laid waste and house will fall against house. And if Satan is divided against himself, how will his kingdom stand? For you say that it is by Beelzebul that I drive out demons. If I, then, drive out demons by Beelzebul, by whom do your own people drive them out? Therefore they will be your judges. But if it is by the finger of God that I drive out demons, then the Kingdom of God has come upon you. When a strong man fully armed guards his palace, his possessions are safe. But when one stronger than he attacks and overcomes him, he takes away the armor on which he relied and distributes the spoils. Whoever is not with me is against me, and whoever does not gather with me scatters."

Friends, in today's Gospel, we learn of a person possessed by a demon. Jesus meets the man and drives out the demon, but then is immediately accused of being in league with Satan. Some of the witnesses said, "By the power of Beelzebul, the prince of demons, he drives out demons."

Jesus' response is wonderful in its logic and laconicism: "Every kingdom divided against itself will be laid waste and house will fall against house. And if Satan is divided against himself, how will his kingdom stand?"

The demonic power is always one of scattering. It breaks up communion. But Jesus, as always, is the voice of *communio*, of one bringing things back together.

Think back to Jesus' feeding of the five thousand. Facing a large, hungry crowd, his disciples beg him to "dismiss the crowds so that they can go to the villages and buy food for themselves." But Jesus answers, "There is no need for them to go away; give them some food yourselves."

Whatever drives the Church apart is an echo of this "dismiss the crowds" impulse, and a reminder of the demonic tendency to divide. In times of trial and threat, this is a very common instinct. We blame, attack, break up, and disperse. But Jesus is right: "There is no need for them to go away."

REFLECT: Are there any parts of the Church that you blame or attack? How can you change your attitude and work for unity among all parts of the Body of Christ?

Friday, March 25, 2022

Solemnity of the Annunciation of the Lord

LUKE 1:26-38

The angel Gabriel was sent from God to a town of Galilee called Nazareth, to a virgin betrothed to a man named Joseph, of the house of David, and the virgin's name was Mary. And coming to her, he said, "Hail, full of grace! The Lord is with you." But she was greatly troubled at what was said and pondered what sort of greeting this might be. Then the angel said to her, "Do not be afraid, Mary, for you have found favor with God. Behold, you will conceive in your womb and bear a son, and you shall name him Jesus. He will be great and will be called Son of the Most High, and the Lord God will give him the throne of David his father, and he will rule over the house of Jacob forever, and of his Kingdom there will be no end." But Mary said to the angel, "How can this be, since I have no relations with a man?" And the angel said to her in reply, "The Holy Spirit will come upon you, and the power of the Most High will overshadow you. Therefore the child to be born will be called holy, the Son of God. And behold, Elizabeth, your relative, has also conceived a son in her old age, and this is the sixth month for her who was called barren; for nothing will be impossible for

God." Mary said, "Behold, I am the handmaid of the Lord. May it be done to me according to your word." Then the angel departed from her.

Friends, in today's Gospel from Luke, we find the Annunciation to Mary. Here is what Gabriel said to the Virgin: "You will conceive in your womb and bear a son, and you shall name him Jesus. . . . The Lord God will give him the throne of David his father, and he will rule over the house of Jacob forever, and of his Kingdom there will be no end."

No first-century Israelite would have missed the meaning here: this child shall be the fulfillment of the promise made to King David.

And this means that the child is, in fact, the King of the world, the one who would bring unity and peace to the nations. The conviction grew upon Israel that this mysterious descendant of David would be king—not just for a time and not just in an earthly sense, but forever and for all nations. This definitive King of the Jews would be King of the world. He would be our King, as well.

REFLECT: How is Jesus the King of your world right now? How can you support the building of his everlasting kingdom?

Saturday, March 26, 2022

Third Week of Lent

LUKE 18:9-14

Jesus addressed this parable to those who were convinced of their own righteousness and despised everyone else. "Two people went up to the temple area to pray; one was a Pharisee and the other was a tax collector. The Pharisee took up his position and spoke this prayer to himself, 'O God, I thank you that I am not like the rest of humanity—greedy, dishonest, adulterous—or even like this tax collector. I fast twice a week, and I pay tithes on my whole income.' But the tax collector stood off at a distance and would not even raise his eyes to heaven but beat his breast and prayed, 'O God, be merciful to me a sinner.' I tell you, the latter went home justified, not the former; for everyone who exalts himself will be humbled, and the one who humbles himself will be exalted."

Friends, today's Gospel compares the self-centered prayer of the Pharisee with the God-centered prayer of the tax collector.

The Pharisee spoke his prayer to himself. This is, Jesus suggests, a fraudulent, wholly inadequate prayer, precisely because it simply confirms the man in his self-regard. And the god to which he prays is, necessarily, a false god, an idol, since it allows itself to be positioned by the ego-driven needs of the Pharisee.

But then Jesus invites us to meditate upon the publican's prayer. He speaks with a simple eloquence: "[He] beat his breast and prayed, 'O God, be merciful to me a sinner.'" Though it is articulate speech, it is not language that confirms the independence and power of the speaker—just the contrary. It is more of a cry or a groan, an acknowledgment that he needs to receive something, this mysterious mercy for which he begs.

In the first prayer, "god" is the principal member of the audience arrayed before the ego of the Pharisee. But in this second prayer, God is the principal actor, and the publican is the audience awaiting a performance the contours of which he cannot fully foresee.

REFLECT: When have you made God in your own image, or in other words, positioned him with your own ego-driven needs?

Sunday, March 27, 2022

Fourth Sunday of Lent

LUKE 15:1-3, 11-32

Tax collectors and sinners were all drawing near to listen to Jesus, but the Pharisees and scribes began to complain, saying, "This man welcomes sinners and eats with them." So to them Jesus addressed this parable: "A man had two sons, and the younger son said to his father, 'Father give me the share of your estate that should come to me.' So the father divided the property between them. After a few days, the younger son collected all his belongings and set off to a distant country where he squandered his inheritance on a life of dissipation. When he had freely spent everything, a severe famine struck that country, and he found himself in dire need. So he hired himself out to one of the local citizens who sent him to his farm to tend the swine. And he longed to eat his fill of the pods on which the swine fed, but nobody gave him any. Coming to his senses he thought, 'How many of my father's hired workers have more than enough food to eat, but here am I, dying from hunger. I shall get up and go to my father and I shall say to him, "Father, I have sinned against heaven and against you. I no longer deserve to be called your son; treat me as you would treat one of your hired workers."'

So he got up and went back to his father. While he was still a long way off, his father caught sight of him, and was filled with compassion. He ran to his son, embraced him and kissed him. His son said to him, 'Father, I have sinned against heaven and against you; I no longer deserve to be called your son.' But his father ordered his servants, 'Quickly bring the finest robe and put it on him; put a ring on his finger and sandals on his feet. Take the fattened calf and slaughter it. Then let us celebrate with a feast, because this son of mine was dead, and has come to life again; he was lost, and has been found.' Then the celebration began. Now the older son had been out in the field and, on his way back, as he neared the house, he heard the sound of music and dancing. He called one of the servants and asked what this might mean. The servant said to him, 'Your brother has returned and your father has slaughtered the fattened calf because he has him back safe and sound.' He became angry, and when he refused to enter the house, his father came out and pleaded with him. He said to his father in reply, 'Look, all these years I served you and not once did I disobey your orders; yet you never gave me even a young goat to feast on with my friends. But when your son returns who swallowed up your property with prostitutes, for him you slaughter the

> fattened calf.' He said to him, 'My son, you are here with me always; everything I have is yours. But now we must celebrate and rejoice, because your brother was dead and has come to life again; he was lost and has been found.'"

Friends, our Gospel today is Jesus' best-known parable, and perhaps the greatest story ever told. It tells us practically everything we need to know about our relationship to God, if we but attend to the details carefully.

The younger son asks for his share of the estate and quickly squanders it in a faraway land—and so it always goes. We are the children of God; we have been given life, being, everything by him; we exist through him at every moment. What is represented here so vividly is the moment of sin, which means rupture or division.

So he was forced to hire himself out so as to become a feeder of pigs. And no one gave him anything. Coming to his senses at last, he decides to break away and return to his father.

The father sees him from a long way off, and then, throwing respectability to the wind, he comes running out to meet him. The Bible is not the story of our quest for God, but of God's passionate, relentless quest for us. He put a ring on his son's finger—the ring of marriage, symbolizing the reestablishment of a right relationship between us and God.

REFLECT: How has God relentlessly pursued you throughout your lifetime?

_____

_____

_____

_____

_____

_____

_____

_____

_____

_____

_____

_____

_____

_____

_____

_____

Monday, March 28, 2022

Fourth Week of Lent

JOHN 4:43-54

At that time Jesus left [Samaria] for Galilee. For Jesus himself testified that a prophet has no honor in his native place. When he came into Galilee, the Galileans welcomed him, since they had seen all he had done in Jerusalem at the feast; for they themselves had gone to the feast.

Then he returned to Cana in Galilee, where he had made the water wine. Now there was a royal official whose son was ill in Capernaum. When he heard that Jesus had arrived in Galilee from Judea, he went to him and asked him to come down and heal his son, who was near death. Jesus said to him, "Unless you people see signs and wonders, you will not believe." The royal official said to him, "Sir, come down before my child dies." Jesus said to him, "You may go; your son will live." The man believed what Jesus said to him and left. While the man was on his way back, his slaves met him and told him that his boy would live. He asked them when he began to recover. They told him, "The fever left him yesterday, about one in the afternoon." The father realized that just at that time Jesus had said to him, "Your son will live," and he and his whole household came to believe. Now this was the second sign Jesus did when he came to Galilee from Judea.

Friends, in today's Gospel, Jesus heals the son of a royal official.

Healer: that's why he's come; that's who he is. In Jesus, divinity and humanity meet. His hands and mouth and eyes, his whole body becomes a conduit of God's energy. What's God's energy, God's purpose? To set right a world gone wrong, a suffering world. Out of every pore of his body, Jesus expresses the healing love of God.

Jesus' ministry of healing expresses in history God's ultimate intention for the world. In Jesus, we see a hint of that world to come where there will be no more suffering, no more sadness, no more sickness.

He does not wait for the sinner, the sufferer, the marginalized to come to him. In love and humility, he goes to them. This same Jesus, risen from the dead, present and alive in the Church, is still seeking us out, coming into our homes—not waiting for us to crawl to him but seeking us out in love and humility.

REFLECT: How do you make yourself open to the healing love of God, which is constantly seeking you? What is necessary before anyone can accept God's love?

Tuesday, March 29, 2022

Fourth Week of Lent

JOHN 5:1-16

There was a feast of the Jews, and Jesus went up to Jerusalem. Now there is in Jerusalem at the Sheep Gate a pool called in Hebrew Bethesda, with five porticoes. In these lay a large number of ill, blind, lame, and crippled. One man was there who had been ill for thirty-eight years. When Jesus saw him lying there and knew that he had been ill for a long time, he said to him, "Do you want to be well?" The sick man answered him, "Sir, I have no one to put me into the pool when the water is stirred up; while I am on my way, someone else gets down there before me." Jesus said to him, "Rise, take up your mat, and walk." Immediately the man became well, took up his mat, and walked.

Now that day was a sabbath. So the Jews said to the man who was cured, "It is the sabbath, and it is not lawful for you to carry your mat." He answered them, "The man who made me well told me, 'Take up your mat and walk.'" They asked him, "Who is the man who told you, 'Take it up and walk'?" The man who was healed did not know who it was, for Jesus had slipped away, since there was a crowd there. After this Jesus found him in the temple area and said to

> him, "Look, you are well; do not sin any more, so that nothing worse may happen to you." The man went and told the Jews that Jesus was the one who had made him well. Therefore, the Jews began to persecute Jesus because he did this on a sabbath.

Friends, in today's Gospel, we find the beautiful healing of a paralyzed man who had been ill for thirty-eight years. Jesus sees the man lying on his mat, next to a pool, and asks, "Do you want to be well?" The man answers him, and Jesus replies, "Rise, take up your mat, and walk." Immediately, the man is healed.

Now at this point, the story really heats up. We notice something that is frequently on display in the Gospels: the resistance to the creative work of God, the attempt to find any excuse, however lame, to deny it, to pretend it's not there, to condemn it.

One would expect that everyone around the cured man would rejoice, but just the contrary: the Jewish leaders are infuriated and confounded. They see the healed man and their first response is, "It is the sabbath, and it is not lawful for you to carry your mat."

Why are they so reactive? Why don't they want this to be? We sinners don't like the ways of God. We find them troubling and threatening. Why? Because they undermine the games of oppression and exclusion that we rely upon in order to boost our own egos.

Let this encounter remind us that God's ways are not our ways, and that there is one even greater than the sabbath.

REFLECT: What did the Jewish leaders focus on and what did they miss or refuse to see? What blinded them?

_____

_____

_____

_____

_____

_____

_____

_____

_____

_____

_____

_____

_____

Wednesday, March 30, 2022

Fourth Week of Lent

JOHN 5:17-30

Jesus answered the Jews:
"My Father is at work until now, so I am at work."
For this reason they tried all the more to kill him,
because he not only broke the sabbath but he also
called God his own father, making himself equal
to God.

Jesus answered and said to them, "Amen, amen, I say
to you, the Son cannot do anything on his own, but
only what he sees the Father doing; for what he does,
the Son will do also. For the Father loves the Son and
shows him everything that he himself does, and he will
show him greater works than these, so that you may
be amazed. For just as the Father raises the dead and
gives life, so also does the Son give life to whomever he
wishes. Nor does the Father judge anyone, but he has
given all judgment to the Son, so that all may honor
the Son just as they honor the Father. Whoever does
not honor the Son does not honor the Father who sent
him. Amen, amen, I say to you, whoever hears my
word and believes in the one who sent me has eternal
life and will not come to condemnation, but has passed
from death to life. Amen, amen, I say to you, the hour
is coming and is now here when the dead will hear

the voice of the Son of God, and those who hear will live. For just as the Father has life in himself, so also he gave to the Son the possession of life in himself. And he gave him power to exercise judgment, because he is the Son of Man. Do not be amazed at this, because the hour is coming in which all who are in the tombs will hear his voice and will come out, those who have done good deeds to the resurrection of life, but those who have done wicked deeds to the resurrection of condemnation.

"I cannot do anything on my own; I judge as I hear, and my judgment is just, because I do not seek my own will but the will of the one who sent me."

Friends, in today's Gospel, we see Jesus as the judge who shows mercy and love. The New Testament sense is that the suffering of the world is produced by the breaking of the loop of grace, the insistence that one's life should be one's own. When this attitude dominates, when we want knowledge of good and evil for ourselves, when we want what is coming to us, we end up losing the little that we think we have.

Jesus saved us by the whole course of his obedience. His Savior's life was an obedient response to the will of God, a displacement of his own concerns in favor of the Father's: "Amen, amen, I say to you, a son cannot do anything on his own, but only what he sees his father doing; for what he does, his son will do also."

REFLECT: When have you displaced your own concerns to prioritize the concerns of God? What difficulties, if any, did you have in doing this?

_____

_____

_____

_____

_____

_____

_____

_____

_____

_____

_____

_____

_____

_____

Thursday, March 31, 2022

Fourth Week of Lent

JOHN 5:31-47

Jesus said to the Jews: "If I testify on my own behalf, my testimony is not true. But there is another who testifies on my behalf, and I know that the testimony he gives on my behalf is true. You sent emissaries to John, and he testified to the truth. I do not accept human testimony, but I say this so that you may be saved. He was a burning and shining lamp, and for a while you were content to rejoice in his light. But I have testimony greater than John's. The works that the Father gave me to accomplish, these works that I perform testify on my behalf that the Father has sent me. Moreover, the Father who sent me has testified on my behalf. But you have never heard his voice nor seen his form, and you do not have his word remaining in you, because you do not believe in the one whom he has sent. You search the Scriptures, because you think you have eternal life through them; even they testify on my behalf. But you do not want to come to me to have life.

"I do not accept human praise; moreover, I know that you do not have the love of God in you. I came in the name of my Father, but you do not accept me; yet if another comes in his own name, you will accept him.

How can you believe, when you accept praise from one another and do not seek the praise that comes from the only God? Do not think that I will accuse you before the Father: the one who will accuse you is Moses in whom you have placed your hope. For if you had believed Moses, you would have believed me, because he wrote about me. But if you do not believe his writings, how will you believe my words?"

Friends, in today's Gospel, Jesus declares the source of his authoritative behavior. Notably, the first hearers of Jesus were astonished by the authority of his speech. This wasn't simply because he spoke with conviction and enthusiasm; it was because he refused to play the game that every other rabbi played, tracing his authority finally back to Moses. He went, as it were, over the head of Moses.

His listeners knew they were dealing with something qualitatively different than anything else in their religious tradition or experience. They were dealing with the prophet greater than Moses, whom Israel had long expected.

And Jesus had to be more than a mere prophet. Why? Because we all have been wounded, indeed our entire world compromised, by a battle that took place at a more fundamental level of existence. The result is the devastation of sin, which we all know too well. Who alone could possibly take it on? A merely human figure?

Hardly. What is required is the power and authority of the Creator himself, intent on remaking and saving his world, binding up its wounds and setting it right.

REFLECT: In this Gospel passage, Jesus said that the works he was doing testified on his behalf that he was sent from the Father. How do your works testify that you are also sent by Jesus on mission?

Friday, April 1, 2022

Fourth Week of Lent

JOHN 7:1-2, 10, 25-30

Jesus moved about within Galilee; he did not wish to travel in Judea, because the Jews were trying to kill him. But the Jewish feast of Tabernacles was near.

But when his brothers had gone up to the feast, he himself also went up, not openly but as it were in secret.

Some of the inhabitants of Jerusalem said, "Is he not the one they are trying to kill? And look, he is speaking openly and they say nothing to him. Could the authorities have realized that he is the Christ? But we know where he is from. When the Christ comes, no one will know where he is from." So Jesus cried out in the temple area as he was teaching and said, "You know me and also know where I am from. Yet I did not come on my own, but the one who sent me, whom you do not know, is true. I know him, because I am from him, and he sent me." So they tried to arrest him, but no one laid a hand upon him, because his hour had not yet come.

Friends, the Gospel for today centers around a theme that we can never speak of enough: the divinity of Jesus. There has been a disturbing tendency in recent years—you can see it clearly in Eckhart Tolle's bestselling book, *The Power of Now*—to turn Jesus into an inspiring spiritual teacher, like the Buddha or the Sufi mystics.

But if that's all he is, the heck with him. The Gospels are never content with such a reductive description. Though they present Jesus quite clearly as a teacher, they know that he is infinitely more than that. They affirm that something else is at stake in him and in our relation to him.

In our Gospel today, Jesus plainly declares his relationship with his Father: "I did not come on my own, but the one who sent me, whom you do not know, is true. I know him, because I am from him, and he sent me."

REFLECT: What sets Jesus apart from other inspiring religious teachers? Does any other religion claim to have a founder and leader with this same characteristic? What does belief in this characteristic compel us to do?

Saturday, April 2, 2022

Fourth Week of Lent

JOHN 7:40-53

Some in the crowd who heard these words of Jesus said, "This is truly the Prophet." Others said, "This is the Christ." But others said, "The Christ will not come from Galilee, will he? Does not Scripture say that the Christ will be of David's family and come from Bethlehem, the village where David lived?" So a division occurred in the crowd because of him. Some of them even wanted to arrest him, but no one laid hands on him.

So the guards went to the chief priests and Pharisees, who asked them, "Why did you not bring him?" The guards answered, "Never before has anyone spoken like this man." So the Pharisees answered them, "Have you also been deceived? Have any of the authorities or the Pharisees believed in him? But this crowd, which does not know the law, is accursed." Nicodemus, one of their members who had come to him earlier, said to them, "Does our law condemn a man before it first hears him and finds out what he is doing?" They answered and said to him, "You are not from Galilee also, are you? Look and see that no prophet arises from Galilee."

Then each went to his own house.

Friends, we see in today's Gospel how Jesus' preaching caused division. Some hearers believed him, but others wanted to arrest him.

The life, preaching, and mission of Jesus are predicated upon the assumption that all is not well with us, that we stand in need of a renovation of vision, attitude, and behavior. A few decades ago the book *I'm OK—You're OK* appeared. Its title, and the attitude that it embodies, are inimical to Christianity.

The fact of sin is so often overlooked today. Look, no one has ever savored being accused of sin, but especially in our culture now, there is an allergy to admitting personal fault.

A salvation religion makes no sense if all is basically fine with us, if all we need is a little sprucing up around the edges. Christian saints are those who can bear the awful revelation that sin is not simply an abstraction or something that other people wrestle with, but a power that lurks and works in them.

When we lose sight of sin, we lose sight of Christianity, which is a salvation religion.

REFLECT: In examining your life and your conscience, in what ways is sin "a power that lurks and works" in you? Or do you have an "allergy to admitting personal fault"?

Sunday, April 3, 2022

Fifth Sunday of Lent

JOHN 8:1-11

Jesus went to the Mount of Olives. But early in the morning he arrived again in the temple area, and all the people started coming to him, and he sat down and taught them. Then the scribes and the Pharisees brought a woman who had been caught in adultery and made her stand in the middle. They said to him, "Teacher, this woman was caught in the very act of committing adultery. Now in the law, Moses commanded us to stone such women. So what do you say?" They said this to test him, so that they could have some charge to bring against him. Jesus bent down and began to write on the ground with his finger. But when they continued asking him, he straightened up and said to them, "Let the one among you who is without sin be the first to throw a stone at her." Again he bent down and wrote on the ground. And in response, they went away one by one, beginning with the elders. So he was left alone with the woman before him. Then Jesus straightened up and said to her, "Woman, where are they? Has no one condemned you?" She replied, "No one, sir." Then Jesus said, "Neither do I condemn you. Go, and from now on do not sin any more."

Friends, today's Gospel presents the story of the woman caught in adultery, which is one of the clearest demonstrations of what René Girard called the scapegoat mechanism.

The scribes and Pharisees bring to Jesus a woman they had caught in adultery. Where must they have been standing and how long must they have been waiting in order to catch her? Their eagerness to find a victim is testimony to the insatiable human need for scapegoats.

The novelty of the Gospel is revealed in Jesus' refusal to contribute to the energy of the gathering storm: "Let the one among you who is without sin be the first to throw a stone at her." Jesus directs the energy of scapegoating violence back toward the accusers. He unveils the dangerous secret that the unstable order of the society has been predicated upon scapegoating. The Church Fathers emphasized this point with a neat interpretive move: they imagined that Jesus was writing in the sand none other than the sins of those who were threatening the woman.

Then we see, at least in seminal form, the new order: "Go, and from now on do not sin any more." The connection between Jesus and the woman is not the consequence of condemnation but rather the fruit of forgiveness offered and accepted.

REFLECT: Reflect on the prevalence of scapegoating in contemporary culture. Think especially about the times when you have been guilty of singling out an individual or some group as a scapegoat.

Monday, April 4, 2022

Fifth Week of Lent

JOHN 8:12-20

Jesus spoke to them again, saying, "I am the light of the world. Whoever follows me will not walk in darkness, but will have the light of life." So the Pharisees said to him, "You testify on your own behalf, so your testimony cannot be verified." Jesus answered and said to them, "Even if I do testify on my own behalf, my testimony can be verified, because I know where I came from and where I am going. But you do not know where I come from or where I am going. You judge by appearances, but I do not judge anyone. And even if I should judge, my judgment is valid, because I am not alone, but it is I and the Father who sent me. Even in your law it is written that the testimony of two men can be verified. I testify on my behalf and so does the Father who sent me." So they said to him, "Where is your father?" Jesus answered, "You know neither me nor my Father. If you knew me, you would know my Father also." He spoke these words while teaching in the treasury in the temple area. But no one arrested him, because his hour had not yet come.

Friends, in our Gospel today, Jesus announces who he is: "I am the light of the world." In John's Gospel there are a series of "I am" statements: "I am the bread of life"; "I am the good shepherd"; "I am the way, the truth, and the life." And here he issues another of those powerful claims: "I am the light."

Christianity is, above all, a way of seeing. Everything else in Christian life flows from and circles around the transformation of vision. Christians see differently, and that is why their prayer, their worship, their action, their whole way of being in the world have a distinctive accent and flavor.

And Jesus is the way to see. When we are grafted onto him, when we assume his mind and his attitude, when we live his life, we are able to see the world as it is, and not through the distorting lens of our fear and our hatred.

REFLECT: How deeply are you grafted onto Jesus? Do you think with his mind or with your own? Do you live his life or your own? How do the outcomes differ depending on how these two questions are answered?

Tuesday, April 5, 2022

Fifth Week of Lent

JOHN 8:21-30

Jesus said to the Pharisees: "I am going away and you will look for me, but you will die in your sin. Where I am going you cannot come." So the Jews said, "He is not going to kill himself, is he, because he said, 'Where I am going you cannot come'?" He said to them, "You belong to what is below, I belong to what is above. You belong to this world, but I do not belong to this world. That is why I told you that you will die in your sins. For if you do not believe that I AM, you will die in your sins." So they said to him, "Who are you?" Jesus said to them, "What I told you from the beginning. I have much to say about you in condemnation. But the one who sent me is true, and what I heard from him I tell the world." They did not realize that he was speaking to them of the Father. So Jesus said to them, "When you lift up the Son of Man, then you will realize that I AM, and that I do nothing on my own, but I say only what the Father taught me. The one who sent me is with me. He has not left me alone, because I always do what is pleasing to him." Because he spoke this way, many came to believe in him.

Friends, in today's Gospel, Jesus prophesies his Crucifixion and his Father's role in his coming death. What enabled the first Christians to hold up the cross, to sing its praises, to wear it as a decoration is the fact that God raised up and ratified precisely this crucified Jesus: "You killed him, but God raised him up." Therefore, God was involved in this terrible thing; God was there, working out his salvific purposes.

But what does this mean? There have been numerous attempts throughout the Christian centuries to name the salvific nature of the cross. Let me offer just one take on it. It became clear to the first Christians that somehow, on that terrible cross, sin had been dealt with. The curse of sin had been removed, taken care of. On that terrible cross, Jesus functioned as the "Lamb of God," sacrificed for sin.

Does this mean God the Father is a cruel taskmaster, demanding a bloody sacrifice so that his anger might be appeased? No, Jesus' Crucifixion was the opening up of the divine heart so that we could see that no sin of ours could finally separate us from the love of God.

REFLECT: What does the Crucifixion of Jesus mean to you personally? Do you believe that through faith in Jesus, no sin of yours will ever separate you from the love of God? How does this faith affect the way you live?

Wednesday, April 6, 2022

Fifth Week of Lent

JOHN 8:31-42

Jesus said to those Jews who believed in him, "If you remain in my word, you will truly be my disciples, and you will know the truth, and the truth will set you free." They answered him, "We are descendants of Abraham and have never been enslaved to anyone. How can you say, 'You will become free'?" Jesus answered them, "Amen, amen, I say to you, everyone who commits sin is a slave of sin. A slave does not remain in a household forever, but a son always remains. So if the Son frees you, then you will truly be free. I know that you are descendants of Abraham. But you are trying to kill me, because my word has no room among you. I tell you what I have seen in the Father's presence; then do what you have heard from the Father."

They answered and said to him, "Our father is Abraham." Jesus said to them, "If you were Abraham's children, you would be doing the works of Abraham. But now you are trying to kill me, a man who has told you the truth that I heard from God; Abraham did not do this. You are doing the works of your father!" So they said to him, "We were not born of fornication. We have one Father,

God." Jesus said to them, "If God were your Father, you would love me, for I came from God and am here; I did not come on my own, but he sent me."

Friends, in today's Gospel, the Lord tells some Jewish leaders that they are enslaved to sin and that the truth will set them free.

Jesus was distinguishing between sins and sin, between the underlying disease and its many symptoms. When the Curé d'Ars was asked what wisdom he had gained about human nature from his many years of hearing confessions, he responded, "People are much sadder than they seem." Blaise Pascal rests his apologetic for Christianity on the simple fact that all people are unhappy. This universal, enduring, and stubborn sadness is sin.

Now, this does not mean that sin is identical to psychological depression. The worst sinners can be the most psychologically well-adjusted people, and the greatest saints can be, by any ordinary measure, quite unhappy.

When I speak of sadness in this context, I mean the deep sense of unfulfillment. We want the truth and we get it, if at all, in dribs and drabs; we want the good, and we achieve it only rarely; we seem to know what we ought to be, but we are in fact something else. This spiritual frustration, this inner warfare, this debility of soul, is sin.

REFLECT: Reflect on the underlying disease of *sin*. Human nature is tainted by this disease and no human, except the Blessed Mother, escapes it. What's the implication of this statement for you personally?

_____

_____

_____

_____

_____

_____

_____

_____

_____

_____

_____

_____

_____

Thursday, April 7, 2022

Fifth Week of Lent

Jesus said to the Jews: "Amen, amen, I say to you, whoever keeps my word will never see death." So the Jews said to him, "Now we are sure that you are possessed. Abraham died, as did the prophets, yet you say, 'Whoever keeps my word will never taste death.' Are you greater than our father Abraham, who died? Or the prophets, who died? Who do you make yourself out to be?" Jesus answered, "If I glorify myself, my glory is worth nothing; but it is my Father who glorifies me, of whom you say, 'He is our God.' You do not know him, but I know him. And if I should say that I do not know him, I would be like you a liar. But I do know him and I keep his word. Abraham your father rejoiced to see my day; he saw it and was glad." So the Jews said to him, "You are not yet fifty years old and you have seen Abraham?" Jesus said to them, "Amen, amen, I say to you, before Abraham came to be, I AM." So they picked up stones to throw at him; but Jesus hid and went out of the temple area.

Friends, today, Jesus refers to himself as "I AM," the name God revealed to Moses. So let's reflect on this episode from Exodus. While tending sheep in the hill country, Moses sees a strange sight. There an angel of the Lord appears to him in fire, flaming out of a bush. God sees him and calls him by name: "Moses, Moses. I am the God of your fathers, the God of Abraham, the God of Isaac, the God of Jacob." This is a very familiar God, one who knows Moses' ancestors.

Moses makes bold to ask, "If the Israelites ask me, 'What is his name?' what am I to tell them?" God replied: "I am who I am." What does that mean? God is saying, in essence, "I cannot be defined, described, or delimited. I am not a being, but rather the sheer act of to-be itself."

"This is what you shall tell the Israelites: I AM sent me to you." The sheer act of being itself cannot be avoided, and it cannot be controlled. It can only be surrendered to in faith. How shocking and strange Jesus' listeners must have found it when Jesus took this name for himself!

REFLECT: How have you tried to avoid or control God, the great I AM?

Friday, April 8, 2022

Fifth Week of Lent

JOHN 10:31-42

The Jews picked up rocks to stone Jesus. Jesus answered them, "I have shown you many good works from my Father. For which of these are you trying to stone me?" The Jews answered him, "We are not stoning you for a good work but for blasphemy. You, a man, are making yourself God." Jesus answered them, "Is it not written in your law, 'I said, 'You are gods'"? If it calls them gods to whom the word of God came, and Scripture cannot be set aside, can you say that the one whom the Father has consecrated and sent into the world blasphemes because I said, 'I am the Son of God'? If I do not perform my Father's works, do not believe me; but if I perform them, even if you do not believe me, believe the works, so that you may realize and understand that the Father is in me and I am in the Father." Then they tried again to arrest him; but he escaped from their power.

He went back across the Jordan to the place where John first baptized, and there he remained. Many came to him and said, "John performed no sign, but everything John said about this man was true." And many there began to believe in him.

Friends, in today's Gospel, Jesus declares, "The Father is in me and I am in the Father."

Charles Williams stated that the master idea of Christianity is "coinherence," mutual indwelling. If you want to see this idea concretely displayed, look to the pages of the Book of Kells, that masterpiece of early Christian illumination. Lines interwoven, designs turning in and around on each other, plays of plants, animals, planets, human beings, angels, and saints. The Germans call it *Ineinander* (one in the other).

How do we identify ourselves? Almost exclusively through the naming of relationships: we are sons, brothers, daughters, mothers, fathers, members of organizations, members of the Church, etc. We might want to be alone, but no one and nothing is finally an island. Coinherence is indeed the name of the game, at all levels of reality.

And God—the ultimate reality—is a family of coinherent relations, each marked by the capacity for self-emptying. Though Father and Son are really distinct, they are utterly implicated in each other by a mutual act of love.

REFLECT: How does thinking about the Trinity as a "family of coinherent relations" shed light on this mystery? What does it say about the importance of loving relationships?

Saturday, April 9, 2022

Fifth Week of Lent

JOHN 11:45-56

Many of the Jews who had come to Mary and seen what Jesus had done began to believe in him. But some of them went to the Pharisees and told them what Jesus had done. So the chief priests and the Pharisees convened the Sanhedrin and said, "What are we going to do? This man is performing many signs. If we leave him alone, all will believe in him, and the Romans will come and take away both our land and our nation." But one of them, Caiaphas, who was high priest that year, said to them, "You know nothing, nor do you consider that it is better for you that one man should die instead of the people, so that the whole nation may not perish." He did not say this on his own, but since he was high priest for that year, he prophesied that Jesus was going to die for the nation, and not only for the nation, but also to gather into one the dispersed children of God. So from that day on they planned to kill him.

So Jesus no longer walked about in public among the Jews, but he left for the region near the desert, to a town called Ephraim, and there he remained with his disciples.

> Now the Passover of the Jews was near, and many went up from the country to Jerusalem before Passover to purify themselves. They looked for Jesus and said to one another as they were in the temple area, "What do you think? That he will not come to the feast?"

Friends, in today's Gospel, the chief priests and Pharisees unite in a plot to kill Jesus because he raised Lazarus from the dead.

The Crucifixion of Jesus is a classic instance of Catholic philosopher René Girard's scapegoating theory. He held that a society, large or small, that finds itself in conflict comes together through a common act of blaming an individual or group purportedly responsible for the conflict.

It is utterly consistent with the Girardian theory that Caiaphas, the leading religious figure of the time, said to his colleagues, "It is better for you that one man should die instead of the people, so that the whole nation may not perish."

In any other religious context, this sort of rationalization would be validated. But in the Resurrection of Jesus from the dead, this stunning truth is revealed: God is not on the side of the scapegoaters, but rather on the side of the scapegoated victim.

The true God does not sanction a community created through violence; rather, he sanctions what Jesus called the kingdom of God, a society grounded in forgiveness, love, and identification with the victim.

REFLECT: How did the scapegoating death of Jesus surprisingly "gather into one the dispersed children of God" (John 11:52)?

Sunday, April 10, 2022

Palm Sunday of the Passion of the Lord

LUKE 22:14–23:56 (OR LUKE 23:1–49)

When the hour came, Jesus took his place at table with the apostles. He said to them, "I have eagerly desired to eat this Passover with you before I suffer, for, I tell you, I shall not eat it again until there is fulfillment in the kingdom of God." Then he took a cup, gave thanks, and said, "Take this and share it among yourselves; for I tell you that from this time on I shall not drink of the fruit of the vine until the kingdom of God comes." Then he took the bread, said the blessing, broke it, and gave it to them, saying, "This is my body, which will be given for you; do this in memory of me." And likewise the cup after they had eaten, saying, "This cup is the new covenant in my blood, which will be shed for you.

"And yet behold, the hand of the one who is to betray me is with me on the table; for the Son of Man indeed goes as it has been determined; but woe to that man by whom he is betrayed." And they began to debate among themselves who among them would do such a deed.

Then an argument broke out among them about which of them should be regarded as the greatest. He said to them, "The kings of the Gentiles lord it over them and those in authority over them are addressed as 'Benefactors'; but among you it shall not be so. Rather, let the greatest among you be as the youngest, and the leader as the servant. For who is greater: the one seated at table or the one who serves? Is it not the one seated at table? I am among you as the one who serves. It is you who have stood by me in my trials; and I confer a kingdom on you, just as my Father has conferred one on me, that you may eat and drink at my table in my kingdom; and you will sit on thrones judging the twelve tribes of Israel.

"Simon, Simon, behold Satan has demanded to sift all of you like wheat, but I have prayed that your own faith may not fail; and once you have turned back, you must strengthen your brothers." He said to him, "Lord, I am prepared to go to prison and to die with you." But he replied, "I tell you, Peter, before the cock crows this day, you will deny three times that you know me."

He said to them, "When I sent you forth without a money bag or a sack or sandals, were you in need of anything?" "No, nothing," they replied. He said to them, "But now one who has a money bag should take it, and likewise a sack, and one who does not have a sword should sell his cloak and buy one. For I tell you that this Scripture must be fulfilled in me, namely, *He was counted among the wicked*; and indeed what is written about me is coming to fulfillment." Then they said, "Lord, look, there are two swords here." But he replied, "It is enough!"

Then going out, he went, as was his custom, to the Mount of Olives, and the disciples followed him. When he arrived at the place he said to them, "Pray that you may not undergo the test." After withdrawing about a stone's throw from them and kneeling, he prayed, saying, "Father, if you are willing, take this cup away from me; still, not my will but yours be done." And to strengthen him an angel from heaven appeared to him. He was in such agony and he prayed so fervently that his sweat became like drops of blood falling on the ground. When he rose from prayer and returned to his disciples, he found them sleeping from grief. He said to them, "Why are you sleeping? Get up and pray that you may not undergo the test."

While he was still speaking, a crowd approached and in front was one of the Twelve, a man named Judas. He went up to Jesus to kiss him. Jesus said to him, "Judas, are you betraying the Son of Man with a kiss?" His disciples realized what was about to happen, and they asked, "Lord, shall we strike with a sword?" And one of them struck the high priest's servant and cut off his right ear. But Jesus said in reply, "Stop, no more of this!" Then he touched the servant's ear and healed him. And Jesus said to the chief priests and temple guards and elders who had come for him, "Have you come out as against a robber, with swords and clubs? Day after day I was with you in the temple area, and you did not seize me; but this is your hour, the time for the power of darkness."

After arresting him they led him away and took him into the house of the high priest; Peter was following at a distance. They lit a fire in the middle of the courtyard and sat around it, and Peter sat down with them. When a maid saw him seated in the light, she looked intently at him and said, "This man too was with him." But he denied it saying, "Woman, I do not know him." A short while later someone else saw him and said, "You too are one of them"; but Peter answered, "My friend, I am not." About an hour later, still another insisted, "Assuredly, this man too was with him, for he also is a Galilean." But Peter said, "My friend, I do not know what you are talking about." Just as he was saying this, the cock crowed, and the Lord turned and looked at Peter; and Peter remembered the word of the Lord, how he had said to him, "Before the cock crows today, you will deny me three times." He went out and began to weep bitterly. The men who held Jesus in custody were ridiculing and beating him. They blindfolded him and questioned him, saying, "Prophesy! Who is it that struck you?" And they reviled him in saying many other things against him.

When day came the council of elders of the people met, both chief priests and scribes, and they brought him before their Sanhedrin. They said, "If you are the Christ, tell us," but he replied to them, "If I tell you, you will not believe, and if I question, you will not respond. But from this time on the Son of Man will be seated at the right hand of the power of God." They all asked, "Are you then the Son of God?" He replied to them, "You say that I am." Then they said, "What further need have we for testimony? We have heard it from his own mouth."

Then the whole assembly of them arose and brought him before Pilate. They brought charges against him, saying, "We found this man misleading our people; he opposes the payment of taxes to Caesar and maintains that he is the Christ, a king." Pilate asked him, "Are you the king of the Jews?" He said to him in reply, "You say so." Pilate then addressed the chief priests and the crowds, "I find this man not guilty." But they were adamant and said, "He is inciting the people with his teaching throughout all Judea, from Galilee where he began even to here."

On hearing this Pilate asked if the man was a Galilean; and upon learning that he was under Herod's jurisdiction, he sent him to Herod who was in Jerusalem at that time. Herod was very glad to see Jesus; he had been wanting to see him for a long time, for he had heard about him and had been hoping to see him perform some sign. He questioned him at length, but he gave him no answer. The chief priests and scribes, meanwhile, stood by accusing him harshly. Herod and his soldiers treated him contemptuously and mocked him, and after clothing him in resplendent garb, he sent him back to Pilate. Herod and Pilate became friends that very day, even though they had been enemies formerly. Pilate then summoned the chief priests, the rulers, and the people and said to them, "You brought this man to me and accused him of inciting the people to revolt. I have conducted my investigation in your presence and have not found this man guilty of the charges you have brought against him, nor did Herod, for he sent him back to us. So no capital crime has been committed by him. Therefore I shall have him flogged and then release him."

But all together they shouted out, "Away with this man! Release Barabbas to us." — Now Barabbas had been imprisoned for a rebellion that had taken place in the city and for murder. — Again Pilate addressed them, still wishing to release Jesus, but they continued their shouting, "Crucify him! Crucify him!" Pilate addressed them a third time, "What evil has this man done? I found him guilty of no capital crime. Therefore I shall have him flogged and then release him." With loud shouts, however, they persisted in calling for his crucifixion, and their voices prevailed. The verdict of Pilate was that their demand should be granted. So he released the man who had been imprisoned for rebellion and murder, for whom they asked, and he handed Jesus over to them to deal with as they wished.

As they led him away they took hold of a certain Simon, a Cyrenian, who was coming in from the country; and after laying the cross on him, they made him carry it behind Jesus. A large crowd of people followed Jesus, including many women who mourned and lamented him. Jesus turned to them and said, "Daughters of Jerusalem, do not weep for me; weep instead for yourselves and for your children for indeed, the days are coming when people will say, 'Blessed are the barren, the wombs that never bore and the breasts that never nursed.' At that time people will say to the mountains, 'Fall upon us!' and to the hills, 'Cover us!' for if these things are done when the wood is green what will happen when it is dry?" Now two others, both criminals, were led away with him to be executed.

When they came to the place called the Skull, they crucified him and the criminals there, one on his right, the other on his left. Then Jesus said, "Father, forgive them, they know not what they do." They divided his garments by casting lots. The people stood by and watched; the rulers, meanwhile, sneered at him and said, "He saved others, let him save himself if he is the chosen one, the Christ of God." Even the soldiers jeered at him. As they approached to offer him wine they called out, "If you are King of the Jews, save yourself." Above him there was an inscription that read, "This is the King of the Jews."

Now one of the criminals hanging there reviled Jesus, saying, "Are you not the Christ? Save yourself and us." The other, however, rebuking him, said in reply, "Have you no fear of God, for you are subject to the same condemnation? And indeed, we have been condemned justly, for the sentence we received corresponds to our crimes, but this man has done nothing criminal." Then he said, "Jesus, remember me when you come into your kingdom." He replied to him, "Amen, I say to you, today you will be with me in Paradise."

It was now about noon and darkness came over the whole land until three in the afternoon because of an eclipse of the sun. Then the veil of the temple was torn down the middle. Jesus cried out in a loud voice, "Father, into your hands I commend my spirit"; and when he had said this he breathed his last.

Here all kneel and pause for a short time.

The centurion who witnessed what had happened glorified God and said, "This man was innocent beyond doubt." When all the people who had gathered for this spectacle saw what had happened, they returned home beating their breasts; but all his acquaintances stood at a distance, including the women who had followed him from Galilee and saw these events.

Now there was a virtuous and righteous man named Joseph who, though he was a member of the council, had not consented to their plan of action. He came from the Jewish town of Arimathea and was awaiting the kingdom of God. He went to Pilate and asked for the body of Jesus. After he had taken the body down, he wrapped it in a linen cloth and laid him in a rock-hewn tomb in which no one had yet been buried. It was the day of preparation, and the sabbath was about to begin. The women who had come from Galilee with him followed behind, and when they had seen the tomb and the way in which his body was laid in it, they returned and prepared spices and perfumed oils. Then they rested on the sabbath according to the commandment.

Friends, how dark are the readings for Palm Sunday! We read through Luke's Passion narrative, leaving out the good news of the Resurrection. To get to the bottom of this emphasis on suffering, to decipher its religious meaning, is to uncover the theological significance of this day.

Do you remember the first time that life really knocked you around? It might have been an extraordinary failure; it might have been the first time you confronted real violence or real hatred; it might have been a massive disappointment; it might have been the death of someone that you loved. This mess, this problem, bedevils all of us.

The biblical approach is clear: God sets about a rescue operation—the formation of a holy people Israel who would follow his commands, worship him aright, and thereby become a magnet to the world. They would teach and show the way out of the dilemma.

He would form a people ready to receive him; he would gradually effect a unity between divinity and humanity; and one day, a servant of Yahweh would appear, someone despised and reviled by men. And this mysterious figure would solve the problem by bearing away the sins of the world, by carrying them off through his suffering.

REFLECT: Reflect on the marvel of God's plan of salvation and how he turns suffering into triumph for all who believe.

Monday, April 11, 2022

Monday of Holy Week

JOHN 12:1-11

Six days before Passover Jesus came to Bethany, where Lazarus was, whom Jesus had raised from the dead. They gave a dinner for him there, and Martha served, while Lazarus was one of those reclining at table with him. Mary took a liter of costly perfumed oil made from genuine aromatic nard and anointed the feet of Jesus and dried them with her hair; the house was filled with the fragrance of the oil. Then Judas the Iscariot, one of his disciples, and the one who would betray him, said, "Why was this oil not sold for three hundred days' wages and given to the poor?" He said this not because he cared about the poor but because he was a thief and held the money bag and used to steal the contributions. So Jesus said, "Leave her alone. Let her keep this for the day of my burial. You always have the poor with you, but you do not always have me."

The large crowd of the Jews found out that he was there and came, not only because of him, but also to see Lazarus, whom he had raised from the dead. And the chief priests plotted to kill Lazarus too, because many of the Jews were turning away and believing in Jesus because of him.

Friends, in today's Gospel, Mary of Bethany anoints Jesus' feet with perfumed oil, preparing him for burial.

This gesture—wasting something as expensive as an entire jar of perfume—is sniffed at by Judas, who complains that, at the very least, the nard could have been sold and the money given to the poor.

Why does John use this tale to preface his telling of the Passion? Why does he allow the odor of this woman's perfume to waft, as it were, over the whole of the story? It is because, I believe, this extravagant gesture shows forth the meaning of what Jesus is about to do: the absolutely radical giving away of self.

There is nothing calculating, careful, or conservative about the woman's action. Flowing from the deepest place in the heart, religion resists the strictures set for it by a fussily moralizing reason (on full display in those who complain about the woman's extravagance). At the climax of his life, Jesus will give himself away totally, lavishly, unreasonably—and this is why Mary's beautiful gesture is a sort of overture to the opera that will follow.

REFLECT: When have you acted "from the deepest place in your heart," fully knowing that someone would seriously disapprove of your actions? What was the result?

_____

_____

_____

_____

Tuesday, April 12, 2022

Tuesday of Holy Week

JOHN 13:21-33, 36-38

Reclining at table with his disciples, Jesus was deeply troubled and testified, "Amen, amen, I say to you, one of you will betray me." The disciples looked at one another, at a loss as to whom he meant. One of his disciples, the one whom Jesus loved, was reclining at Jesus' side. So Simon Peter nodded to him to find out whom he meant. He leaned back against Jesus' chest and said to him, "Master, who is it?" Jesus answered, "It is the one to whom I hand the morsel after I have dipped it." So he dipped the morsel and took it and handed it to Judas, son of Simon the Iscariot. After Judas took the morsel, Satan entered him. So Jesus said to him, "What you are going to do, do quickly." Now none of those reclining at table realized why he said this to him. Some thought that since Judas kept the money bag, Jesus had told him, "Buy what we need for the feast," or to give something to the poor. So Judas took the morsel and left at once. And it was night.

When he had left, Jesus said, "Now is the Son of Man glorified, and God is glorified in him. If God is glorified in him, God will also glorify him in himself, and he will glorify him at once. My children, I will be with you only a little while longer. You will look for me, and as I told the Jews, 'Where I go you cannot come,' so now I say it to you."

Simon Peter said to him, "Master, where are you going?" Jesus answered him, "Where I am going, you cannot follow me now, though you will follow later." Peter said to him, "Master, why can I not follow you now? I will lay down my life for you." Jesus answered, "Will you lay down your life for me? Amen, amen, I say to you, the cock will not crow before you deny me three times."

Friends, in today's Gospel, Jesus foretells the denial of Peter, which is fulfilled in the account of the Passion. Peter later denies Jesus three times before the cock crows and, remembering Jesus' prediction, breaks down and weeps.

After the Resurrection, Peter and the other disciples returned to Galilee to work as fishermen again, and there spotted Jesus on the far shore. As Jesus draws Peter back into his circle of intimacy, we witness a beautiful act of spiritual direction. Three times the Lord asks Peter whether he loves him, and three times Peter affirms it: "Lord, you know that I love you."

St. Augustine was the first to comment that the threefold statement of love was meant to counteract the threefold denial.

Peter emerges as the archetype of the forgiven and commissioned Church, for after each of his reaffirmations, Peter hears the command to tend the sheep. Once we are brought back into friendship with Jesus, we are called to love those whom he loves.

REFLECT: Reflect on this and other Gospel stories about Peter. In what ways is he an appropriate archetype of the Church?

Wednesday, April 13, 2022

Wednesday of Holy Week

MATTHEW 26:14-25

One of the Twelve, who was called Judas Iscariot, went to the chief priests and said, "What are you willing to give me if I hand him over to you?" They paid him thirty pieces of silver, and from that time on he looked for an opportunity to hand him over.

On the first day of the Feast of Unleavened Bread, the disciples approached Jesus and said, "Where do you want us to prepare for you to eat the Passover?" He said, "Go into the city to a certain man and tell him, 'The teacher says, "My appointed time draws near; in your house I shall celebrate the Passover with my disciples."'" The disciples then did as Jesus had ordered, and prepared the Passover.

When it was evening, he reclined at table with the Twelve. And while they were eating, he said, "Amen, I say to you, one of you will betray me." Deeply distressed at this, they began to say to him one after another, "Surely it is not I, Lord?" He said in reply, "He who has dipped his hand into the dish with me is the one who will betray me. The Son of Man indeed goes, as it is written of him, but woe to that man by whom the Son of Man is betrayed. It would be better for that man if he had never been born."

> Then Judas, his betrayer, said in reply, "Surely it is not I, Rabbi?" He answered, "You have said so."

Friends, in today's Gospel, Jesus asks his disciples to go into Jerusalem and prepare a Passover supper.

At the heart of the Passover meal was the eating of a lamb, which had been sacrificed, in remembrance of the lambs of the original Passover, whose blood had been smeared on the doorposts of the Israelites in Egypt. Making his Last Supper a Passover meal, Jesus was signaling the fulfillment of John the Baptist's prophecy that he, Jesus, would be the Lamb of God and the definitive sacrifice.

This sacrifice is made sacramentally present at every Mass—not for the sake of God, who has no need of it, but for our sake. In the Mass, we participate in the act by which divinity and humanity are reconciled, and we eat the sacrificed body and drink the poured-out blood of the Lamb of God.

REFLECT: How does partaking in the Body and Blood of Jesus at Mass affect you?

_____

_____

_____

_____

Thursday, April 14, 2022

Holy Thursday: Evening Mass of the Lord's Supper

Before the feast of Passover, Jesus knew that his hour had come to pass from this world to the Father. He loved his own in the world and he loved them to the end. The devil had already induced Judas, son of Simon the Iscariot, to hand him over. So, during supper, fully aware that the Father had put everything into his power and that he had come from God and was returning to God, he rose from supper and took off his outer garments. He took a towel and tied it around his waist. Then he poured water into a basin and began to wash the disciples' feet and dry them with the towel around his waist. He came to Simon Peter, who said to him, "Master, are you going to wash my feet?" Jesus answered and said to him, "What I am doing, you do not understand now, but you will understand later." Peter said to him, "You will never wash my feet." Jesus answered him, "Unless I wash you, you will have no inheritance with me." Simon Peter said to him, "Master, then not only my feet, but my hands and head as well." Jesus said to him, "Whoever has bathed has no need except to have his feet washed, for he is clean all over; so you are clean, but not all." For he knew who would betray him; for this reason, he said, "Not all of you are clean."

> So when he had washed their feet and put his garments back on and reclined at table again, he said to them, "Do you realize what I have done for you? You call me 'teacher' and 'master,' and rightly so, for indeed I am. If I, therefore, the master and teacher, have washed your feet, you ought to wash one another's feet. I have given you a model to follow, so that as I have done for you, you should also do."

Friends, in today's Gospel, Jesus washes the disciples' feet. He is giving them a visual proclamation of his new commandment: "Love one another. As I have loved you, so you also should love one another."

When we accept this commandment, we walk the path of joy. When we internalize this law, we become happy. And so the paradox: happiness is never a function of filling oneself up; it is a wonderful function of giving oneself away.

When the divine grace enters one's life (and everything we have is the result of divine grace), the task is to contrive a way to make it a gift. In a sense, the divine life—which exists only in gift form—can be "had" only on the fly.

Notice please that we are to love with a properly divine love: "I have called you friends, because I have told you everything I have heard from my Father." Radical, radical, radical. Complete, excessive, over-the-top.

REFLECT: What have you received out of divine love? How are you giving it away?

_____

_____

_____

_____

_____

_____

_____

_____

_____

_____

_____

_____

_____

_____

_____

_____

Friday, April 15, 2022

Good Friday

Jesus went out with his disciples across the Kidron valley to where there was a garden, into which he and his disciples entered. Judas his betrayer also knew the place, because Jesus had often met there with his disciples. So Judas got a band of soldiers and guards from the chief priests and the Pharisees and went there with lanterns, torches, and weapons. Jesus, knowing everything that was going to happen to him, went out and said to them, "Whom are you looking for?" They answered him, "Jesus the Nazorean." He said to them, "I AM." Judas his betrayer was also with them. When he said to them, "I AM," they turned away and fell to the ground. So he again asked them, "Whom are you looking for?" They said, "Jesus the Nazorean." Jesus answered, "I told you that I AM. So if you are looking for me, let these men go." This was to fulfill what he had said, "I have not lost any of those you gave me." Then Simon Peter, who had a sword, drew it, struck the high priest's slave, and cut off his right ear. The slave's name was Malchus. Jesus said to Peter, "Put your sword into its scabbard. Shall I not drink the cup that the Father gave me?"

So the band of soldiers, the tribune, and the Jewish guards seized Jesus, bound him, and brought him to Annas first. He was the father-in-law of Caiaphas, who was high priest that year. It was Caiaphas who had counseled the Jews that it was better that one man should die rather than the people.

Simon Peter and another disciple followed Jesus. Now the other disciple was known to the high priest, and he entered the courtyard of the high priest with Jesus. But Peter stood at the gate outside. So the other disciple, the acquaintance of the high priest, went out and spoke to the gatekeeper and brought Peter in. Then the maid who was the gatekeeper said to Peter, "You are not one of this man's disciples, are you?" He said, "I am not." Now the slaves and the guards were standing around a charcoal fire that they had made, because it was cold, and were warming themselves. Peter was also standing there keeping warm.

The high priest questioned Jesus about his disciples and about his doctrine. Jesus answered him, "I have spoken publicly to the world. I have always taught in a synagogue or in the temple area where all the Jews gather, and in secret I have said nothing. Why ask me? Ask those who heard me what I said to them.

They know what I said." When he had said this, one of the temple guards standing there struck Jesus and said, "Is this the way you answer the high priest?" Jesus answered him, "If I have spoken wrongly, testify to the wrong; but if I have spoken rightly, why do you strike me?" Then Annas sent him bound to Caiaphas the high priest.

Now Simon Peter was standing there keeping warm. And they said to him, "You are not one of his disciples, are you?" He denied it and said, "I am not." One of the slaves of the high priest, a relative of the one whose ear Peter had cut off, said, "Didn't I see you in the garden with him?" Again Peter denied it. And immediately the cock crowed.

Then they brought Jesus from Caiaphas to the praetorium. It was morning. And they themselves did not enter the praetorium, in order not to be defiled so that they could eat the Passover. So Pilate came out to them and said, "What charge do you bring against this man?" They answered and said to him, "If he were not a criminal, we would not have handed him over to you." At this, Pilate said to them, "Take him yourselves, and judge him according to your law." The Jews answered him, "We do not have the right to execute anyone," in order that the word of Jesus might be fulfilled that he said indicating the kind of death he would die. So Pilate went back into the praetorium and summoned Jesus and said to him, "Are you the King of the Jews?" Jesus answered, "Do you say this on your own or have others told you about me?" Pilate answered, "I am not a Jew, am I? Your own nation and the chief priests handed you over to me. What have you done?" Jesus answered, "My kingdom does not belong to this world. If my kingdom did belong to this world, my attendants would be fighting to keep me from being handed over to the Jews. But as it is, my kingdom is not here." So Pilate said to him, "Then you are a king?" Jesus answered, "You say I am a king. For this I was born and for this I came into the world, to testify to the truth. Everyone who belongs to the truth listens to my voice." Pilate said to him, "What is truth?"

When he had said this, he again went out to the Jews and said to them, "I find no guilt in him. But you have a custom that I release one prisoner to you at Passover. Do you want me to release to you the King of the Jews?" They cried out again, "Not this one but Barabbas!" Now Barabbas was a revolutionary.

Then Pilate took Jesus and had him scourged. And the soldiers wove a crown out of thorns and placed it on his head, and clothed him in a purple cloak, and they came to him and said, "Hail, King of the Jews!" And they struck him repeatedly. Once more Pilate went out and said to them, "Look, I am bringing him out to you, so that you may know that I find no guilt in him." So Jesus came out, wearing the crown of thorns and the purple cloak. And he said to them, "Behold, the man!" When the chief priests and the guards saw him they cried out, "Crucify him, crucify him!" Pilate said to them, "Take him yourselves and crucify him. I find no guilt in him." The Jews answered, "We have a law, and according to that law he ought to die, because he made himself the Son of God." Now when Pilate heard this statement, he became even more afraid, and went back into the praetorium and said to Jesus, "Where are you from?" Jesus did not answer him. So Pilate said to him, "Do you not speak to me? Do you not know that I have power to release you and I have power to crucify you?" Jesus answered him, "You would have no power over me if it had not been given to you from above. For this reason the one who handed me over to you has the greater sin." Consequently, Pilate tried to release him; but the Jews cried out, "If you release him, you are not a Friend of Caesar. Everyone who makes himself a king opposes Caesar."

When Pilate heard these words he brought Jesus out and seated him on the judge's bench in the place called Stone Pavement, in Hebrew, Gabbatha. It was preparation day for Passover, and it was about noon. And he said to the Jews, "Behold, your king!" They cried out, "Take him away, take him away! Crucify him!" Pilate said to them, "Shall I crucify your king?" The chief priests answered, "We have no king but Caesar." Then he handed him over to them to be crucified.

So they took Jesus, and, carrying the cross himself, he went out to what is called the Place of the Skull, in Hebrew, Golgotha. There they crucified him, and with him two others, one on either side, with Jesus in the middle. Pilate also had an inscription written and put on the cross. It read, "Jesus the Nazorean, the King of the Jews." Now many of the Jews read this inscription, because the place where Jesus was crucified was near the city; and it was written in Hebrew, Latin, and Greek. So the chief priests of the Jews said to Pilate, "Do not write 'The King of the Jews,' but that he said, 'I am the King of the

Jews.'" Pilate answered, "What I have written, I have written."

When the soldiers had crucified Jesus, they took his clothes and divided them into four shares, a share for each soldier. They also took his tunic, but the tunic was seamless, woven in one piece from the top down. So they said to one another, "Let's not tear it, but cast lots for it to see whose it will be," in order that the passage of Scripture might be fulfilled that says:
> *They divided my garments among them,*
> *and for my vesture they cast lots.*

This is what the soldiers did. Standing by the cross of Jesus were his mother and his mother's sister, Mary the wife of Clopas, and Mary of Magdala. When Jesus saw his mother and the disciple there whom he loved he said to his mother, "Woman, behold, your son." Then he said to the disciple, "Behold, your mother." And from that hour the disciple took her into his home.

After this, aware that everything was now finished, in order that the Scripture might be fulfilled, Jesus said, "I thirst." There was a vessel filled with common wine. So they put a sponge soaked in wine on a sprig of hyssop and put it up to his mouth. When Jesus had taken the wine, he said, "It is finished." And bowing his head, he handed over the spirit.

Here all kneel and pause for a short time.

Now since it was preparation day, in order that the bodies might not remain on the cross on the sabbath, for the sabbath day of that week was a solemn one, the Jews asked Pilate that their legs be broken and that they be taken down. So the soldiers came and broke the legs of the first and then of the other one who was crucified with Jesus. But when they came to Jesus and saw that he was already dead, they did not break his legs, but one soldier thrust his lance into his side, and immediately blood and water flowed out. An eyewitness has testified, and his testimony is true; he knows that he is speaking the truth, so that you also may come to believe. For this happened so that the Scripture passage might be fulfilled:

Not a bone of it will be broken.

And again another passage says:

They will look upon him whom they have pierced.

After this, Joseph of Arimathea, secretly a disciple of Jesus for fear of the Jews, asked Pilate if he could remove the body of Jesus. And Pilate permitted it. So he came and took his body. Nicodemus, the one who had first come to him at night, also came bringing a mixture of myrrh and aloes weighing about one hundred pounds. They took the body of Jesus and bound it with burial cloths along with the spices, according to the Jewish burial custom. Now in the place where he had been crucified there was a garden, and in the garden a new tomb, in which no one had yet been buried. So they laid Jesus there because of the Jewish preparation day; for the tomb was close by.

Friends, today's Gospel is John's wonderful narrative of Christ's Passion.

On the cross, Jesus entered into close quarters with sin (because that's where we sinners are found) and allowed the heat and fury of sin to destroy him, even as he protected us.

We can see, with special clarity, why the first Christians associated the crucified Jesus with the suffering servant of Isaiah. By enduring the pain of the cross, Jesus did indeed bear our sins; by his stripes we were indeed healed.

And this is why the sacrificial death of Jesus is pleasing to the Father. The Father sent his Son into godforsakenness, into the morass of sin and death—not because he delighted in seeing his

Son suffer, but rather because he wanted his Son to bring the divine light to the darkest place.

It is not the agony of the Son in itself that pleases his Father, but rather the Son's willing obedience in offering his body in sacrifice in order to take away the sin of the world. St. Anselm said that the death of the Son reestablished the right relationship between divinity and humanity.

REFLECT: What did Jesus love and what did he hate while on the cross? How will you seek to love and hate the same things?

Saturday, April 16, 2022

Holy Saturday

LUKE 24:1-12

At daybreak on the first day of the week the women who had come from Galilee with Jesus took the spices they had prepared and went to the tomb. They found the stone rolled away from the tomb; but when they entered, they did not find the body of the Lord Jesus. While they were puzzling over this, behold, two men in dazzling garments appeared to them. They were terrified and bowed their faces to the ground. They said to them, "Why do you seek the living one among the dead? He is not here, but he has been raised. Remember what he said to you while he was still in Galilee, that the Son of Man must be handed over to sinners and be crucified, and rise on the third day." And they remembered his words. Then they returned from the tomb and announced all these things to the eleven and to all the others. The women were Mary Magdalene, Joanna, and Mary the mother of James; the others who accompanied them also told this to the apostles, but their story seemed like nonsense and they did not believe them. But Peter got up and ran to the tomb, bent down, and saw the burial cloths alone; then he went home amazed at what had happened.

Friends, how wonderful are the readings for the Easter season! So full of theological depth, so spiritually rich, so marked by joy.

In light of the Resurrection, we know that God's deepest intention for us is life, and life to the full. He wants death not to have the final word; he wants a renewal of the heavens and the earth.

Therefore, we have to stop living in the intellectual and spiritual space of death. We have to stop living intellectually in a world dominated by death and the fear of death. We have to adjust our attitudes in order to respond properly to what God really intends for us and the world.

Though we rarely admit it, we live in a death-haunted space. The fear of death broods over us like a cloud and conditions all of our thoughts and actions. What if we really believed, deep down, that death did not have the final word? Would we live in such fear, in such a cramped spiritual space? Or would we see that the protection of our egos is not the number-one concern of our existence?

REFLECT: How do you honestly feel about your own death? Do you succumb to the culture's way of ignoring death? Do you fear death?

_____

_____

_____

_____

_____

Sunday, April 17, 2022

Easter Sunday of the Resurrection of the Lord

JOHN 20:1-9

On the first day of the week, Mary of Magdala came to the tomb early in the morning, while it was still dark, and saw the stone removed from the tomb. So she ran and went to Simon Peter and to the other disciple whom Jesus loved, and told them, "They have taken the Lord from the tomb, and we don't know where they put him." So Peter and the other disciple went out and came to the tomb. They both ran, but the other disciple ran faster than Peter and arrived at the tomb first; he bent down and saw the burial cloths there, but did not go in. When Simon Peter arrived after him, he went into the tomb and saw the burial cloths there, and the cloth that had covered his head, not with the burial cloths but rolled up in a separate place. Then the other disciple also went in, the one who had arrived at the tomb first, and he saw and believed. For they did not yet understand the Scripture that he had to rise from the dead.

Friends, our Easter Gospel contains St. John's magnificent account of the Resurrection. It was, says John, early in the morning on the first day of the week. It was still dark—just the way it was at the beginning of time before God said, "Let there be light." But a light was about to shine, and a new creation was about to appear.

The stone had been rolled away. That stone, blocking entrance to the tomb of Jesus, stands for the finality of death. When someone that we love dies, it is as though a great stone is rolled across them, permanently blocking our access to them. And this is why we weep at death—not just in grief but in a kind of existential frustration.

But for Jesus, the stone had been rolled away. Undoubtedly, the first disciples must have thought a grave robber had been at work. But the wonderful Johannine irony is that the greatest of grave robbers had indeed been at work. The Lord says to the prophet Ezekiel, "I [will] open your graves and have you rise from them."

What was dreamed about, what endured as a hope against hope, has become a reality. God has opened the grave of his Son, and the bonds of death have been shattered forever.

REFLECT: Although the story is told only on Easter Sunday, how does the Resurrection imbue your daily life with hope?

STATIONS OF

THE CROSS

REFLECTIONS

To watch the video and download the audio version
of these Stations of the Cross, visit:

Stations.WordOnFire.org

The biblical verses in the Stations of the Cross Reflections were transcribed
from Bishop Barron's oral presentation and may not match a specific
translation exactly.

Jesus Is Condemned to Death

When Israel dreamed of a new David, it dreamed of a king who would unite the nation, cleanse the temple, defeat Israel's enemies, and then reign over the whole world. It's only against this loamy backdrop that we can appreciate what Jesus was doing and how he was perceived. The first words out of his mouth— and the central theme of his preaching—concerned the kingdom of God. He announced a new reign, centered on himself.

These were taken, quite rightly, as fighting words, for if a new kingdom is to come, the old kingdoms have to give way, and if a new King has arrived, the old kings have to cede. Jesus endeavored to unite the nation, to bring the tribes back together. This was the point of his open-table fellowship, his reaching out to sinners and tax collectors, his inclusion of the sick and the marginalized. In David's city, he cleansed the temple and promised that he would establish a new temple. And throughout his life and ministry, Jesus opposed the old kings. We see it from the very beginning, in the infancy narratives themselves. Jesus is presented as an alternative to Quirinius and Augustus, and his arrival, even as a baby, is enough to frighten Herod and all Jerusalem.

This confrontation between the old and new orders comes to its highest expression as Jesus stands before Pontius Pilate, the local representative of Caesar. Pilate, undoubtedly sure of his power and authority, sizes up this criminal: "Are you the King of the Jews?" Pilate means this in a purely political and worldly way: "Are you trying to seize political control of this part of the Roman empire?" But the scene is packed with irony, for any Jew would have known the full import of Pilate's question. He was really asking: "Are you the king of the world? Are you the new David, destined to reign over all of the nations?"

Jesus tells him, straightforwardly enough, "My kingdom does not belong to this world." This does not mean that Jesus is unconcerned for the realities of politics, with the very "this-worldly" concerns of justice, peace, and right order. It means that the reign that he has been announcing is not a new political order, based like the others on threats and violence. This is why he immediately clarifies that his attendants are not "fighting to keep me from being handed over." It is the reign of God that he announces, God's nonviolent and compassionate ordering of things. Unimpressed, Pilate asks, "What is truth?" And then he condemns Jesus to death. He plays the typical worldly game of power politics, and by all appearances, he wins, as ruthless and violent people seem to do.

But through the cross and Resurrection, Jesus defeated him. He outmaneuvered the violence of sin and swallowed it up in the divine forgiveness. He defeated the enemies of Israel. And he thereby established his own body as the new temple—which is why blood and water flowed out from it. He gathered all people to himself, as the Davidic king was expected to: "When the Son of Man is raised up, he will draw all people to himself." He was, in short, the new King, the one to whom final allegiance is due.

Jesus Takes Up His Cross

All of us sinners tend to see the universe turning around our egos, our needs, our projects, our plans, our likes and dislikes. True conversion—the *metanoia* that Jesus talks about—is so much more than moral reform, though it includes that. It has to do with a complete shift in consciousness, a whole new way of looking at one's life.

Jesus offered a teaching that must have been gut-wrenching to his first-century audience: "If anyone wishes to come after me, he must deny himself and take up his cross daily and follow me." His listeners knew what the cross meant: a death in utter agony, nakedness, and humiliation. They knew it in all of its awful power.

So why does the Son take up the cross? Because God the Father is angry? Because he wants to lord it over us? Because God needs something? No, he comes purely out of love, out of God's desire that we flourish: "God so loved the world that he gave his only Son, so that everyone who believes in him might not perish but might have eternal life." God the Father is not a pathetic divinity whose bruised personal honor needs to be restored; rather, God is a parent who burns with compassion for his children who have wandered into danger. Does the Father hate sinners? No, but he hates sin. Does he harbor indignation at the unjust? No, but he despises injustice. And thus he sends his Son—not to see him suffer but to set things right. St. Anselm, the great medieval theologian who is often unfairly blamed for the cruel theology of satisfaction, was eminently clear on this score. We sinners are like diamonds that have fallen into the muck; made in the image of God, we have soiled ourselves through violence and hatred. In his passion to reestablish the beauty of his creation, God came down into the muck of sin and death and brought the diamond up and polished it off. In so doing, of course, he had to get dirty. This sinking into the dirt—this divine solidarity with the lost—is the "sacrifice" that the Son makes to the infinite pleasure of the Father. It is a sacrifice expressive not of anger or vengeance but of compassion.

If God is self-forgetting love even to the point of death, then we must be such love. If God is willing to break open his own heart, then we must be willing to break open our hearts for others. The cross, in short, must become the very structure of the Christian life.

There's a line from the illuminator of the St. John's Bible that states: "We have to love our way out of this." There's nothing wimpy or namby-pamby or blind about this conviction. When we love extravagantly, we are not purposely blinding ourselves to moral realities—just the contrary. Love is not a sentiment but "a harsh and dreadful thing," as Dostoevsky said.

This is just what Jesus shows on his terrible cross. And this is just what we, his followers, must imitate. Taking up the cross means not just being willing to suffer but being willing to suffer as he did, absorbing violence and hatred through our forgiveness and nonviolence.

Jesus Falls for the First Time

O n the way to Calvary, Jesus—the Son of God—fell under the weight of the cross.

Some years ago, I delivered a homily on the subject of God's benevolent and providential direction of the cosmos. I felt the sermon had been inspiring and informative, and the numerous people who complimented me afterward confirmed my own assessment. But after everybody else had streamed past me, an older man approached, and eyeing me warily, said, "Father, I'm on a quest, and your homily didn't help." I responded, "Well, what do you mean?"

He then proceeded to tell me a terrible story. He had two granddaughters, ages five and seven, both of whom were suffering from a terminal disease that the doctors could neither control nor fully understand. All they knew for sure was that both girls would die and that, before death, both would go blind. He told me that the elder child had just lost her sight and that the younger was lying awake at night crying in terror as she contemplated her own future. "Father," he said, "my quest is to find out why God is doing this to my granddaughters. I've been to priests, ministers, rabbis, and gurus, and I've never gotten a very good answer— and frankly, your homily shed very little light." Well, I was flabbergasted, stunned. Never had the problem of evil—reconciling the goodness of God with the presence of suffering—appeared to me so concretely and in such a challenging way.

I told him that I didn't have a concrete answer to his question, but that his question itself was a holy one, because it meant that he had not given up on God. He was still searching for God. And if you follow that question all the way, you'll be led to the heart of the Christian mystery, which is that God the Father sends his Son into the very worst of our suffering, into what frightens us the most. And in that we have the answer—not necessarily one that satisfies our curiosity completely, but a deeply powerful spiritual answer: that God doesn't take away our suffering, but he enters into it with us and thereby sanctifies it.

Jesus Meets His Blessed Mother

The Passion of the Christ was one of the most provocative and popular religious movies in decades. One thing that especially struck me when I saw it is the role played by Mary, the mother of Jesus. We are compelled to see the scenes through her eyes. Early in Luke's Gospel, we are told that Mary "contemplated these things, reflecting on them in her heart." She is the theologian par excellence. She is the one who understands.

If Mary is the one through whom Christ was born, and if the Church is indeed Christ's Mystical Body, then she must be, in a very real sense, the Mother of the Church. She is the one through whom Jesus continues to be born. We hear in the Gospel that, as he was dying on the cross, Jesus looked to his mother and the disciple whom he loved, and he said to Mary, "Woman, behold, your son," then to John, "Behold, your mother." We are told that "from that hour the disciple took her into his home." This text supports an ancient tradition that the Apostle John would have taken Mary with him when he traveled to Ephesus in Asia Minor and that both ended their days in that city. Indeed, on the top of a high hill overlooking the Aegean Sea, just outside of Ephesus, there's a modest dwelling that tradition holds to be the house of Mary. Immaculate Mary, the Mother of God, assumed body and soul into heaven, is not of merely historical or theoretical interest, nor is she simply a spiritual exemplar. Instead, as "Queen of all the saints," Mary is an ongoing presence, an actor in the life of the Church. In entrusting Mary to John, Jesus was, in a real way, entrusting Mary to all those who would be friends of Jesus down through the ages.

This is not to confuse her, of course, with the Savior, but it is to insist on her mission as mediator and intercessor. At the close of the great "Hail Mary" prayer, we Catholics ask Mary to pray for us "now and at the hour of our death," signaling that throughout one's life, Mary is the privileged channel through which the grace of Christ flows into the Mystical Body. Her basic task is always to draw people into deeper fellowship with her son. The Church's conviction is that the Blessed Mother continues to say yes to God and to "go in haste" on mission around the world. She does so usually in quiet, hidden ways, responding to prayer and interceding for the Church. But sometimes she does so in a remarkable manner, breaking into our world strikingly and visibly.

God delights in drawing secondary causes into the dense complexity of his providential plan, granting to them the honor of cooperating with him and his designs. The Virgin Mary, the handmaid of the Lord, is the humblest of these humble instruments—and therefore, the most effective.

Simon of Cyrene Is Made to Help Jesus Bear the Cross

A donkey is a beast of burden: a humble, simple, unassuming animal, used by very ordinary people to do their work. The wealthy and powerful might own horses or a team of oxen; a political leader might ride a stately steed; but they would have little to do with donkeys.

All of his public career, Jesus had resisted when people claimed Messiahship for him. He sternly ordered them to be silent. When they came to carry him off and make him king, he slipped away. But on Palm Sunday, he is willing to be proclaimed—precisely at the moment when he rides into Jerusalem on a donkey. And the Gospel is clear: it is a colt, the foal of a donkey, on whom no one had ever previously sat. In other words, this is a young, inexperienced, unimpressive donkey. And this is the animal upon whom Jesus rides into town in triumph.

The humble donkey, pressed into service, is a model of discipleship. Our purpose in life is not to draw attention to ourselves, to have a brilliant career, to aggrandize our egos; rather, our purpose is to serve the Master's need, to cooperate with his work as he sees fit. What was the donkey's task? He was a Christopher, a Christ-bearer. He carried the Lord into Jerusalem, paving the way for the Passion and the redemption of the world. Would anyone have particularly noticed him? Probably not, except perhaps to laugh at this ludicrous animal. What is the task of every disciple? Just the same: to be a Christopher, a bearer of Christ to the world. Might we be unnoticed in this? Sure. Might we, if we are noticed, be laughed at? Well, of course. But the Master has need of us, and so we perform our essential task in the theo-drama.

During Christ's Passion, there is one figure who imitates the donkey, and that's Simon of Cyrene. The Romans didn't want Jesus to die before the Crucifixion. And so they pressed into service (how like the donkey!) a man from Cyrene, in North Africa, probably a visitor coming to Jerusalem for the Passover.

How perilous and dangerous this must have seemed to him! But he seizes the moment and carries the cross, bearing some of Jesus' suffering. Simon of Cyrene must have had many other plans for his life, many other dreams and ambitions. But at the moment of truth, the Master had need of him—and he responded.

And his story is told to this day. "Life is what happens to you while you're busy making other plans." Your life is not about you. Remember: the Master has need of you. Whether and how you respond is all that matters.

Veronica Wipes the Face of Jesus

Tradition has it that a woman called Veronica wiped the blood and sweat from Jesus' face as he made his way to Calvary, leaving his image miraculously imprinted on her veil.

What do we see in the face of Christ? We see the Son of God, the divine Word made flesh. To use Paul's language, God has brought to light "the knowledge of the glory of God on the face of Jesus Christ." In and through his humble humanity, his divinity shines forth. The proximity of his divinity in no way compromises the integrity of his humanity but rather makes it shine in greater beauty. This is the New Testament version of the burning bush. The Jesus who is both divine and human is the Jesus who is evangelically compelling. If he is only divine, then he doesn't touch us; if he is only human, he can't save us. His splendor consists in the coming together of the two natures. This is the Christ who wants to reign as Lord of our lives in every detail.

And we see, in the veil of Veronica, the suffering Lamb of God who takes away the sins of the world. The Lord of Life came, and we killed him. Therefore hiding, denying, covering up, pretense, excuses, subterfuges—all the ruses of self-justification—are permanently out of the question. Our own dysfunction is on public view in every wound on the body of Jesus. When we direct ourselves toward the brilliance of the crucified Christ, every smudge on the windowpane of the soul becomes visible. In the tormented face of the suffering Christ, we know that something has gone terribly wrong with us; that no one is okay; that we're like prisoners chained inside of an escape-proof prison; that we are at war with ourselves; that Pharaoh has enslaved the Israelites and pressed them into service; that we are under judgment; that all we can do is cry, "O Come, O Come, Emmanuel."

But in that veil of Veronica, we also see the face of mercy. When we had wandered into the cold and distant country of sin, God's love came to search us out; when we had sunk under the waves, that love went deeper; when we had closed ourselves up in the somber cave of our self-regard and self-reproach, that love crouched down and, with a candle, entered in. And this is why we Christians don't hide the awful face of the dying Christ. This is why we show it to the world. In Jesus' agonies, God is taking our agony away. We know it is no longer we who live but Christ who lives in us; we realize that nothing can ever separate us from the love of God. The Church doesn't have a mission; it is a mission, and its purpose is to cause the merciful face of Jesus to gaze upon everyone in the world.

Jesus Falls for the Second Time

Under the crushing weight of the cross, Jesus fell a second time.

The prophet Jeremiah gave voice to a longing and a hope that must have been deeply planted in the collective consciousness of the nation. He expresses Yahweh's own pledge that he himself would one day fulfill the covenant and forgive the sins of the people. In the thirty-first chapter of the book of Jeremiah, we find these extraordinary words: "The days are surely coming, says the Lord, when I will make a new covenant with the house of Israel and the house of Judah. It will not be like the covenant I made with their ancestors . . . a covenant that they broke. . . . But this is the covenant that I will make with the house of Israel after those days. . . . I will put my law within them, and I will write it on their hearts; and I will be their God and they will be my people." All the prophets know that the covenants God made with Israel—through Abraham, Moses, and David—have failed, due to the people's infidelity. But Jeremiah dreams that one day, through Yahweh's own direct intervention, a faithful Israel will emerge, a people who have a heart for the Lord, who consider the Law not an external imposition but a joy.

How will this renewal take place? How will Yahweh plant the Law so deeply in the children of Israel that their fulfillment of the covenant will be effortless? To find the answers, we must turn to some mysterious texts in the book of the prophet Isaiah, texts that particularly fascinated the first Christians. In the fifty-second chapter of Isaiah, we find a reference to a figure called "the servant of the Lord," who, we are told, "will be exalted and lifted up and shall be very high." The nations of the earth will see him in this prominent position, but they shall not be looking at a splendid warrior or a majestic victor. Instead, they will be astonished at how "marred was his appearance, beyond human semblance." In chapter fifty-three, the description of this servant continues: "He had no form or majesty that we should look at him, nothing in his appearance that we should desire him. He was despised and rejected by others, a man of suffering and acquainted with infirmity." And then the reason for his deformation and anguish is made clearer: "Surely, he has borne our infirmities and carried our diseases. . . . He was wounded for our transgressions, crushed for our iniquities . . . and the Lord has laid on him the iniquity of us all."

The "suffering servant" is presented, in short, as a sacrificial figure, one who will, on behalf of the entire nation, offer himself for the sins of the many. His greatness will consist not in personal independence and political power but rather in his willingness to bear the weight of sin, to disempower sin, as it were, from within. In a word, the covenant of which Jeremiah speaks (the writing of the Law in the hearts of the people) would be effected through the sacrificial servant of whom Isaiah speaks.

Jesus Meets the Women of Jerusalem

As Jesus is led to Calvary, a great number followed him, including weeping women of Jerusalem. Jesus turned to them and spoke as judge of the world, saying, "Daughters of Jerusalem, do not weep for me, but weep for yourselves and for your children."

The New Testament insists that Jesus both shows us that we are sinners (he is judge) and offers us the way out of sin (he is savior). When one or the other of these emphases is lost, our spiritual path is decisively compromised, either through overconfidence or through terror. When they are both adequately stressed, our spiritual path opens up, because we know we must walk it and we can walk it.

In Jesus of Nazareth, God's own mind became flesh—that is to say, the pattern of God's being appeared in time and space. Colossians tells us that Jesus is the "perfect image," the *eikon*, of the Father. And thus, his arrival was in itself a challenge to all that is not in conformity with the divine pattern. In his very person is the kingdom, the divine *ordo*, and therefore his presence is the light in which the disorder of all the earthly kingdoms becomes apparent. In this sense, his every move, his every word, his every gesture, constituted God's judgment on the world, for in the measure that he was opposed, he clarified the dysfunctional nature of his opponents. When John the Baptist spoke of the coming of the Messiah, he used an edgy image: "His winnowing fork is in his hand, to clear his threshing floor and to gather the wheat into the granary; but the chaff he will burn with unquenchable fire." The farmer in first-century Palestine would place the newly harvested wheat on the floor of the barn and then, using a sort of pitchfork, would toss the grain in the air, forcing the lighter chaff to separate itself from the usable wheat. Thus Jesus' presence would be a winnowing fan, an agent of separation and clarification.

And nowhere is this judgment more evident than in his violent death. Jesus did not simply pass away; he was killed, executed by command of the Roman governor and with the approval of the religious establishment. As Peter put it in the earliest kerygmatic preaching in the Acts of the Apostles: "And you killed the Author of life, whom God raised from the dead." The implication of Peter's speech, of course, is that you, the killers, have been revealed as the enemies of life. And the "you," as Peter himself knew with special insight, included not simply the Roman and Jewish ruling classes, but everyone, even Jesus' most intimate followers.

All the social groups of Jesus' time—Pharisees, Sadducees, Zealots, Essenes, temple priests, Roman occupiers, Christian disciples—had this in common: they were, at the end of the day, opposed to Jesus. At the moment of truth, "they all fled." Bob Dylan said, "The enemy I see / wears the cloak of decency." A favorite ruse of sinners is to wrap themselves in the mantle of respectability; Jesus the judge is the one who rips away the cloak, literally unveiling, "revealing" the truth of things. Whenever we are tempted to think that all is well with us, we hold up the cross of Jesus and let our illusions die.

Jesus Falls for the Third Time

Why did Jesus bear the terrible weight of the cross—a cross so heavy it caused him to fall not once, not twice, but three times?

Because if the weight of sin had been addressed only from a distance, only through divine fiat, it would not have been truly conquered; but when it is withstood by someone willing fully to submit to it, it is effectively exploded from within, undermined, defeated. This is the strategy of Jesus, the Lamb of God.

We see it in a number of Gospel scenes where Jesus is tired out after his contact with the sick, the lost, the sinful. At the beginning of Mark's Gospel, we find an account of a typical day in the ministry of Jesus. The people press on him from all sides, compelling him to find refuge in a boat lest he be crushed by the crowd, and at one point there are so many supplicants surrounding him that he couldn't even eat. Mark tells us that Jesus went off to a secluded place to pray, but even there they sought him out, coming at him from all sides.

In the magnificent narrative of the woman at the well in the Gospel of John, we hear that Jesus sat down by Jacob's well, "tired out by his journey." This description is straightforward enough on the literal level: Who wouldn't be tired after a morning's march through dry country? But as Augustine and others have reminded us, it has another sense on the mystical level. Jesus is tired from his incarnational journey into human sin and dysfunction, signified by the well. "You come to this well every day and you become thirsty again," Jesus says to the woman, indicating that the well is emblematic of errant desire, her tendency to fill up her longing for God with the transient goods of creation: money, pleasure, power, honor. In order to effect a change in her, the Lamb of God had to be willing to enter into her dysfunctional world and to share the spiritual weariness of it. J.R.R. Tolkien keenly appreciated this sacrificial dynamic. His great Christ-figure, Frodo the hobbit, brought about the salvation of Middle-earth precisely through his entry into the heart of the land of Mordor, disempowering that terrible place through his humble willingness to bear the full weight of its burden.

All of this was, however, but an anticipation of the ultimate sacrifice of the Lamb of God. The final enemy that had to be defeated, if God and his human family could once again sit down in easy fellowship, was death itself. In a very real sense, death—and the fear of death—stand behind all sin, and hence Jesus had to journey into the realm of death and, through sacrifice, twist it back to life. Innumerable heroes in the course of human history had tried to conquer that realm by using its weapons, fighting violence with violence and hatred with hatred. But this strategy was (and still is) hopeless. The battle plan of the Lamb of God was paradoxical in the extreme: he would conquer death precisely by dying.

Jesus Is Stripped of His Garments

The soldiers took Jesus' clothes and divided them into four shares, a share for each soldier, and cast lots for his tunic, fulfilling the words of the Psalms: "They divided my garments among them, and for my vesture they cast lots." Christ is stripped of everything: reputation, comfort, esteem, food, drink—even the pathetic clothes on his back.

Thomas Aquinas said that if you want to see the perfect exemplification of the Beatitudes, you should look to Christ crucified. He specified this observation as follows: if you want beatitude (happiness), despise what Jesus despised on the cross and love what he loved on the cross.

What did he despise on the cross but the four classical addictions—wealth, pleasure, power, and honor? At the root of sin is fear, especially fear of death. To counter that fear, people aggrandize the ego, decorating it with the approval of others or stuffing it with worldly goods. But the crucified Jesus was utterly detached from wealth and worldly goods. He was stripped naked, and his hands, fixed to the wood of the cross, could grasp at nothing. More to it, he was detached from pleasure. On the cross, Jesus underwent the most agonizing kind of physical torment, a pain that was literally excruciating (*ex cruce*, from the cross), but he also experienced the extreme of psychological and even spiritual suffering. And he was bereft of power, even to the point of being unable to move or defend himself in any way. Finally, on that terrible cross, he was completely detached from the esteem of others. In a public place not far from the gate of Jerusalem, he hung from an instrument of torture, exposed to the mockery of the crowd, displayed as a common criminal. In this, he endured the limit case of dishonor. In the most dramatic way possible, therefore, the crucified Jesus demonstrated a liberation from the four principal temptations that lead us from God. St. Paul expressed this accomplishment in typically vivid language: "He nailed our sins to the cross."

But what did Jesus love on the cross? He loved the will of his Father. His Father had sent him into the farthest reaches of godforsakenness in order to bring the divine love even to that darkest place, and Jesus loved that mission to the very end. And it was precisely his detachment from the four great temptations that enabled him to walk that walk. What he loved and what he despised were in a strange balance on the cross. Poor in spirit, meek, mourning, and persecuted, he was able to be pure of heart, to seek righteousness utterly, to become the ultimate peacemaker, and to be the perfect conduit of the divine mercy to the world. Though it is supremely paradoxical to say so, the crucified Jesus is, therefore, the man of beatitude, a truly happy man. And Jesus, stripped of his garments and nailed to the cross, is the very icon of liberty, for he is free from those attachments that would prevent him from attaining the true good, which is doing the will of his Father.

Jesus Is Crucified

On the cross, Jesus said, "Father, forgive them, for they know not what they do." Dying on a Roman instrument of torture, he allowed the full force of the world's hatred and dysfunction to wash over him, to spend itself on him. And he responded not with an answering violence or resentment, but with forgiveness. He therefore took away the sin of the world (to use the language of the liturgy), swallowing it up in the divine mercy.

In the Gospel of Luke, Jesus compared himself to a mother hen who longed to gather her chicks under her wing. As N.T. Wright points out, this is much more than a sentimental image. It refers to the gesture of a hen when fire is sweeping through the barn. In order to protect her chicks, she will sacrifice herself, gathering them under her wing and using her own body as a shield. On the cross, Jesus used, as it were, his own sacrificed body as a shield, taking the full force of the world's hatred and violence. He entered into close quarters with sin (because that's where we sinners are found) and allowed the heat and fury of sin to destroy him, even as he protected us. With this metaphor in mind, we can see, with special clarity, why the first Christians associated the crucified Jesus with the suffering servant of Isaiah. By enduring the pain of the cross, Jesus did indeed bear our sins; by his stripes we were indeed healed.

Through the final sacrifice of Jesus the high priest, eternal life has been made available to the whole of humanity. The sacrifice of the Mass is a participation in this great eternal act by which Jesus entered on our behalf into the heavenly sanctuary with his own blood and returned bearing the forgiveness of the Father. When the high priest came out of the sanctuary and sprinkled the people with blood, he was understood to be acting in the very person of Yahweh, renewing creation. The ultimate sacrifice having been offered, Christ the priest comes forth at every Mass with his lifeblood, and the universe is restored. The priest's actions at the altar are but a symbolic manifestation of this mystical reality, which is why he is described as operating *in persona Christi* (in the person of Christ).

Though the ordained priest alone can preside at the Mass and effect the Eucharistic change, all of the baptized participate in the Mass in a priestly way. They do this through their prayers and responses but also, as *Lumen Gentium* specifies, by uniting their personal sacrifices and sufferings to the great sacrifice of Christ. So a father witnesses the agony of his son in the hospital; a mother endures the rebellion of a teenage daughter; a young man receives news of his brother's death in battle; an elderly man tosses on his bed in anxiety as he contemplates his unsure financial situation; a graduate student struggles to complete his doctoral thesis; a child experiences for the first time the breakup of a close friendship; an idealist confronts the stubborn resistance of a cynical opponent. These people could see their pain as simply dumb suffering, the offscourings of an indifferent universe. Or they could see them through the lens provided by the sacrificial death of Jesus, appreciating them as the means by which God is drawing them closer to himself.

Jesus Dies on the Cross

In Mark's Gospel, the last thing we hear from Jesus is an animal cry: "Jesus gave a loud cry and breathed his last." But in John's Gospel, in which the priesthood of Jesus is consistently emphasized, we find, just before Jesus' death, a liturgical word. In the Latin version of this passage, it is *consummatum est*: it is completed. This is the affirmation that a work has been done, that something has been brought to fulfillment. How often in the New Testament do we hear the language of fulfillment: "in order that the Scriptures might be fulfilled" and "in fulfillment of the Scriptures." Jesus saw himself as the climax of a story, as the culminating chapter in a novel, as the hinge of a great drama. If we don't know the contours of the drama, we won't know him.

And the drama involves a rescue operation that God launched by forming the people of Israel after his own heart. When the world had gone wrong through sin, God endeavored to fashion a family that would know him and would worship him aright. This process began with Abraham and the covenant that God cut with him. It continued through Moses and David, as God secured further covenants with them. He wanted to form a priestly people, a people of orthodoxy, right praise. This rightly-ordered people would then become a magnet to the other nations of the world: "Mt. Zion, true pole of the earth, there all the tribes go up, the tribes of the Lord." Though God was ever faithful, the people Israel wavered. Though they were called back by the prophets to covenant fidelity, they did not listen. Though the temple was established as the place of right praise, it became corrupt. And Israel was not the magnet for the other nations but rather their footstool and servant. Israel was enslaved by Egypt, overrun by Assyria, Babylon, Greece, and Rome. More to it, the tribes of Israel, instead of coming together around Mt. Zion, had been scattered. And so Israel began to dream of a new King David, a figure who would fulfill all of its expectations and complete God's rescue operation.

The author of John's Gospel was a master of irony, and one of his most delicious twists involves the sign that Pontius Pilate placed over the cross of the dying Jesus: *Iesus Nazarenus Rex Iudaeorum* (Jesus of Nazareth, King of the Jews). The Roman governor, of course, meant it as a taunt, but the sign—written out in the three major languages of that time and place, Hebrew, Latin, and Greek—in fact made Pilate, unwittingly, the first great evangelist. The king of the Jews, on the Old Testament reading, was destined to be the king of the world—and this is precisely what Pilate effectively announced. Even at Calvary, when it had dwindled to three members, Jesus' Church, his community, was catholic, for it was destined to embrace everyone. At Pentecost, the disciples, gathered in the Upper Room, were filled with the Holy Spirit and began to preach the Good News. They were heard, miraculously, in the many languages of those who had gathered in Jerusalem for the Feast of Tabernacles. As the Church Fathers clearly saw, this was the reversal of the curse of Babel, when the one language of the human race was divided and the people, accordingly, set against each other. Now, through the announcement of the Lordship of Jesus, the many languages again become one, for this message is the one that every person, across space and time, was born to hear: Jesus is the new King.

Jesus Is Taken Down from the Cross and Laid in the Arms of Mary

After the Crucifixion, Jesus was taken from the cross and laid in the arms of Mary—a scene famously captured in Michelangelo's iconic *Pietà*.

For five centuries now, scholars and admirers have remarked the serenity and youthfulness of Mary's face in the *Pietà*. Mary, we presume, would have been at least forty-five or fifty at the time of the Crucifixion. And yet, Michelangelo depicts her as a young woman, perhaps in her early twenties.

What Michelangelo was showing us is not only the historical Mary, but Mary as New Eve, an ever-young Mother of the Church. Michelangelo was, throughout his life, a great devotee of the poet Dante. At the end of the *Divine Comedy* we find a famous line, placed on the lips of St. Bernard as he sings the praises of the Mother of God: "Virgin mother, daughter of your Son, humbled, and exalted, more than any other creature." Since Mary's son, according to the flesh, is also the divine Word through whom all things are made, Mary is indeed both mother and daughter of Christ. Michelangelo suggested this absolutely unique relationship in the youthfulness of Jesus' mother.

One of the most extraordinary features of the *Pietà*, from a purely structural or compositional standpoint, is how Michelangelo managed to make the figures of Jesus and Mary look so natural and elegant together, despite the fact that what is being presented is a woman supporting the body of an adult man on her lap. In fact, Mary's body is significantly larger than that of Jesus. She contains him. In the wonderful words of Sister Wendy

Beckett, she's like a great mountain, and his body is like a river flowing down. The Church Fathers compared Mary to the ark of the covenant, the receptacle of the Ten Commandments, which the ancient Israelites appreciated as the dwelling place of God. So Mary, who carried the incarnate Word in her very womb, becomes the Ark of the Covenant par excellence.

According to the Gospel accounts, Mary, having given birth to Jesus, placed him in a manger, the place where the animals eat. At the climax of his life, Jesus would become food for the life of the world. Michelangelo depicts Mary's left hand in a gesture of offering, as though she is presenting him as a gift. (This same gesture is found in that especially evocative scene in *The Passion of the Christ* when Mary, marked with Jesus' blood, presents the sacrifice of her Son to us and for us.) Her right hand supports him but touches him only indirectly, through her garment. Both are Eucharistic references. The Church continually offers the Body of Jesus under the forms of bread and wine. And when the priest shows the Blessed Sacrament, he touches the monstrance only through a veil. Keep in mind that the sculpture was intended to be an altarpiece—that is to say, something closely associated with the celebration of the Mass. What we see in the *Pietà*, the image of the Virgin Mother cradling her Son, is what we see at the Mass—namely, the offering of the body of the crucified Jesus for the life of the world.

Jesus Is Laid in the Tomb

Joseph of Arimathea, a secret admirer of Jesus, came courageously to ask for the body of the Lord, and a group of women who had accompanied Jesus from Galilee watched carefully to see where he was buried. As his enemies closed in on him and even his most intimate disciples fled in fear, these people stayed with Jesus until the end. Luke aptly speaks of the women as having "followed" the body of Jesus to its resting place, their discipleship of the Lord complete and consistent. Jesus wants to go to the cross because he loves his Father's will; and therefore, those who love him—who want what he wants—go to that same bitter end. In St. John's Gospel, we hear that Jesus is buried in a new tomb that was situated in a garden, which signals the renewal of Eden, the way back into the garden from which we were exiled through sin.

The three women come as we might expect any visitor to any grave to come: they have their oil with them, and they intend to honor the body of Jesus. We might imagine them sitting in reverential silence afterward, reflecting on the life and words of their friend, expressing their admiration for him and the tragedy of his death.

But this is no ordinary grave. The first thing they notice is the stone rolled away. Now, this could have been the result of grave-robbers, of someone trying to break in and desecrate the tomb. It is just beginning to dawn on them that it is the result of someone breaking out.

Then it says, "They made their way out and fled from the tomb bewildered and trembling, and because of their great fear, they said nothing to anyone." This grave is not the source of peace and rest, calm and thoughtful meditation. This grave is the source of terror and upheaval. Ordinary graves are places of finality and inevitability; this grave is a place of novelty so shocking that it frightens the wits out of people. From this grave of Jesus, we learn that the supposed laws of nature aren't laws after all, that what always moved this way now moves that way. Some people think that they will make the Resurrection more intelligible, more acceptable to modern people, if they allegorize it away, turning it into a vague symbol of the perdurance of Jesus' cause. But then his grave wouldn't be frightening; it would be, like the grave of any ordinary hero, sad, wistful, reassuring.

Evangelization—the proclamation of the Good News, the Gospel, the *euangelion*—has to do with the Resurrection of Jesus Christ from the dead. On every page of the New Testament, one can discern an excitement born of something utterly novel and unexpected: that Jesus of Nazareth, who had died on a cross and was buried in a tomb, was, through the power of God, raised up.

Everything else in Christian life flows from and is related to this empty tomb.

All Stations of the Cross images are from the Church of All Saints in Blato, Korcula Island, Croatia.

Conclusion

Friends,

In the name of the Risen Lord, greetings! Lent is over and we've now moved into Easter. Alleluia!

I'd like to thank you for joining me on this journey through the Lenten season. Now that we've finished, you might be wondering, what's next? How do I maintain the spiritual momentum I developed during Lent? I'd like to suggest a few practical tips.

First, be sure to visit our website, **WordOnFire.org**, on a regular basis. There you'll find lots of helpful resources, including new articles, videos, blog posts, podcasts, and homilies, all designed to help strengthen your faith and evangelize the culture. The best part is that all of it is free!

In addition to those free resources, I invite you to join our new Word on Fire Institute. This is an online hub of deep spiritual and intellectual formation, where you'll journey through courses taught by me and other Fellows. Our goal is to build an army of evangelists, people who have been transformed by Christ and want to bring his light to the world. Learn more and sign up at **https://wordonfire.institute.**

Finally, consider carrying on your Lenten progress by grounding your life more concretely in the Eucharist, which is what keeps us alive spiritually. Are you only attending Mass on Sundays?

Commit to attending one extra Mass each week. Is there a chapel nearby that offers Eucharistic Adoration? Sign up for a weekly hour of meditation and prayer before the Blessed Sacrament. The Eucharist is the alpha and the omega of Christian discipleship. It is the energy without which authentic Christianity runs down.

Again, thank you from all of us at Word on Fire, and God bless you during this Easter season!

Peace,

+ Robert Barron

Bishop Robert Barron